This book belongs to:

_____

Introductions by Helen Mort

Compiled by Helen Mort and Jonny Marx

Edited by Jonny Marx

Illustrations by Valeria Valenza

Cover illustration and design by John Bigwood

First published in Great Britain in 2014 by Buster Books,
an imprint of Michael O'Mara Books Limited,
9 Lion Yard, Tremadoc Road, London SW4 7NQ

 www.busterbooks.co.uk Buster Children's Books @BusterBooks

A CIP catalogue record for this book is available from the British Library.

ISBN: 978-1-78055-258-3

1 3 5 7 9 10 8 6 4 2

Printed and bound in August 2014 by CPI Group (UK) Ltd, 108 Beddington
Lane, Croydon, CR0 4YY, United Kingdom.

Papers used by Buster Books are natural, recyclable products made
from wood grown in sustainable forests. The manufacturing processes
conform to the environmental regulations of the country of origin.

The Owl and the Pussycat

Buster Books

Introduction

Poems want you to read them. They want you to remember what they have to say. So read the poems in this book aloud. Shout them across a beach on a windy day. Whisper them in the library. Scribble them on a note and pass it to someone else. Write your favourite line on a windowpane on a rainy day. Take these poems on a bus. Take them for a walk (they're less trouble than a dog). Giggle them, recite them, look at them in silence. As soon as you turn over the page and start to read, these words are all yours.

A poet named Don Paterson says a poem is 'a little machine for remembering itself'. He means, I think, that once you read a poem you like, you can make it your own. You can carry it round in your pocket or even in your head wherever you go.

When I started thinking about which poems should be in this book, I asked my friends about poems they had loved when they were younger. The response bowled me over. Everyone I spoke to didn't just have one favourite poem but a list a mile long. In fact, some of them needed a lorry to contain all the poems they loved. A lot of them could still remember some by heart, too.

I thought about the poems I first read, poems like 'The Owl and the Pussycat' and 'Jabberwocky'. I remembered what they sounded like and how I wanted to read them by torchlight when I was supposed to be asleep in bed. I still feel the same way about poems now that I'm a so-called 'grown up'.

This anthology is called 'Poems Every Child Should Read'. But if you shuffle the words around you get 'Every Child Should Read Poems' (and 'Poems Should Read Every Child', and 'Should Read Every Child Poems', but you get the picture …). The idea that every person will find something that inspires them if they read poetry is something I truly believe.

This anthology shows just how many different shapes and sizes poems come in. Some are old, some are very new. Some rhyme and some don't. Some are funny, some are sad. Some are big, some are small. But they're all there for you to explore and enjoy. If you come across any words about poetry that are new to you, have a look in the glossary at the back of the book where you'll find a quick definition of everything from 'alliteration' to 'sonnet'. Keep your eyes peeled for these little devices and tools and see if you can spot them in action in some of the poems and pages.

Helen Mort

Helen Mort was born in Sheffield in 1985, and grew up in nearby Chesterfield. Five-times winner of the Foyle Young Poets award, she received an Eric Gregory Award from The Society of Authors in 2007 and won the Manchester Young Writer Prize in 2008. In 2010, she became the youngest ever poet in residence at The Wordsworth Trust, Grasmere. Her first collection of poetry, *Division Street*, was shortlisted for the 2013 Costa Poetry Award and the T S Eliot Prize. Helen lives in Derbyshire.

Contents

Animals 7

Nature and the Seasons 37

Monsters, Beasts and Fairies 54

Humour and Nonsense 70

Love and Beauty 91

Hodgepodge Poems 103

Adventure and Exploration 121

War and Death 133

Growing Up 146

History and Legend 163

Acknowledgements 178

Glossary of Poetic Terms 180

Index of Authors 182

Index of Titles 183

Index of First Lines 185

Index of Well-Known Lines 187

Animals

The Owl and the Pussycat

Edward Lear

(1812–1888)

Edward Lear is often described as a 'nonsense poet', which means he wasn't afraid to make up new words when he wanted. In this, his most famous poem, he makes up the word 'runcible spoon', which now appears in many dictionaries. What words would you add to the language if you could?

★★★

The Owl and the Pussycat went to sea
    In a beautiful pea-green boat,
They took some honey, and plenty of money,
    Wrapped up in a five-pound note.
The Owl looked up to the stars above,
    And sang to a small guitar,
'O lovely Pussy! O Pussy, my love,
    What a beautiful Pussy you are,
        You are,
        You are!
What a beautiful Pussy you are!'

Pussy said to the Owl, 'You elegant fowl!
    How charmingly sweet you sing!
O let us be married! too long we have tarried:
    But what shall we do for a ring?'

They sailed away, for a year and a day,
    To the land where the Bong-tree grows
And there in a wood a Piggy-wig stood,
    With a ring at the end of his nose,
        His nose,
        His nose,
With a ring at the end of his nose.

'Dear Pig, are you willing to sell for one shilling
    Your ring?' Said the Piggy, 'I will.'
So they took it away, and were married next day
    By the Turkey who lives on the hill.
They dined on mince, and slices of quince,
    Which they ate with a runcible spoon;
And hand in hand, on the edge of the sand,
    They danced by the light of the moon,
        The moon,
        The moon,
They danced by the light of the moon.

The Ants

John Clare
(1793–1864)

What wonder strikes the curious, while he views
The black ant's city, by a rotten tree,
Or woodland bank! In ignorance we muse:
Pausing, annoy'd, – we know not what we see,
Such government and thought there seem to be;
Some looking on, and urging some to toil,
Dragging their loads of bent-stalks slavishly:
And what's more wonderful, when big loads foil
One ant or two to carry, quickly then
A swarm flock round to help their fellow-men.
Surely they speak a language whisperingly,
Too fine for us to hear; and sure their ways
Prove they have kings and laws, and that they be
Deformed remnants of the Fairy-days.

Snake

D H Lawrence
(1885–1930)

This poem contains something called 'personification' – this term is used when a writer assigns human thoughts, qualities, traits and emotions to animals, nature or objects. How many human characteristics can you spot in Lawrence's description of the snake?

★★★

A snake came to my water-trough
On a hot, hot day, and I in pyjamas for the heat,
To drink there.

In the deep, strange-scented shade of the great dark
    carob-tree
I came down the steps with my pitcher
And must wait, must stand and wait, for there he was at the
    trough before me.

He reached down from a fissure in the earth-wall in
    the gloom
And trailed his yellow-brown slackness soft-bellied down,
    over the edge of the stone trough
And rested his throat upon the stone bottom,
And where the water had dripped from the tap, in a small
    clearness,

He sipped with his straight mouth,
Softly drank through his straight gums, into his slack long body,
Silently.

Someone was before me at my water-trough,
And I, like a second comer, waiting.

He lifted his head from his drinking, as cattle do,
And looked at me vaguely, as drinking cattle do,
And flickered his two-forked tongue from his lips, and mused
    a moment,
And stooped and drank a little more,
Being earth-brown, earth-golden from the burning bowels of
    the earth
On the day of Sicilian July, with Etna smoking.

The voice of my education said to me
He must be killed,
For in Sicily the black, black snakes are innocent, the gold are
    venomous.

And voices in me said, If you were a man
You would take a stick and break him now, and finish him off.

But must I confess how I liked him,
How glad I was he had come like a guest in quiet, to drink at
    my water-trough
And depart peaceful, pacified, and thankless,
Into the burning bowels of this earth?

Was it cowardice, that I dared not kill him?
Was it perversity, that I longed to talk to him?
Was it humility, to feel so honoured?
I felt so honoured.

And yet those voices:
If you were not afraid, you would kill him!

And truly I was afraid, I was most afraid,
But even so, honoured still more
That he should seek my hospitality
From out the dark door of the secret earth.

He drank enough
And lifted his head, dreamily, as one who has drunken,
And flickered his tongue like a forked night on the air, so black;
Seeming to lick his lips,
And looked around like a god, unseeing, into the air,
And slowly turned his head,
And slowly, very slowly, as if thrice adream,
Proceeded to draw his slow length curving round
And climb again the broken bank of my wall-face.

And as he put his head into that dreadful hole,
And as he slowly drew up, snake-easing his shoulders, and
    entered farther,
A sort of horror, a sort of protest against his withdrawing into
    that horrid black hole,

Deliberately going into the blackness, and slowly drawing
    himself after,
Overcame me now his back was turned.

I looked round, I put down my pitcher,
I picked up a clumsy log
And threw it at the water-trough with a clatter.

I think it did not hit him,
But suddenly that part of him that was left behind convulsed
    in undignified haste.
Writhed like lightning, and was gone
Into the black hole, the earth-lipped fissure in the wall-front,
At which, in the intense still noon, I stared with fascination.

And immediately I regretted it.
I thought how paltry, how vulgar, what a mean act!
I despised myself and the voices of my accursed human
    education.

And I thought of the albatross
And I wished he would come back, my snake.

For he seemed to me again like a king,
Like a king in exile, uncrowned in the underworld,
Now due to be crowned again.

And so, I missed my chance with one of the lords
Of life.
And I have something to expiate:
A pettiness.

The Mock Turtle's Song

Lewis Carroll
(1832–1898)

This poem comes from *Alice's Adventures in Wonderland*, a story
which you might know about a girl who falls down a rabbit hole
and finds herself in a world of strange creatures. She meets a blue
caterpillar who smokes a pipe, a white rabbit who is always late, the
Queen of Hearts and a Cheshire cat with a big grin. One of the other
creatures Alice meets on her travels is the mock turtle. He says he used
to be a real turtle and sings Alice a peculiar song. Would you join the
mock turtle's dance?

★★★

'Will you walk a little faster?' said a whiting to a snail,
'There's a porpoise close behind us, and he's treading on
    my tail.
See how eagerly the lobsters and the turtles all advance!
They are waiting on the shingle – will you come and join the
    dance?
Will you, won't you, will you, won't you, will you join the
    dance?
Will you, won't you, will you, won't you, won't you join the
    dance?

'You can really have no notion how delightful it will be
When they take us up and throw us, with the lobsters, out
    to sea!'

But the snail replied 'Too far, too far!', and gave a look
    askance –
Said he thanked the whiting kindly, but he would not join
    the dance.
Would not, could not, would not, could not, would not join
    the dance.
Would not, could not, would not, could not, could not join
    the dance.

'What matters it how far we go?' his scaly friend replied.
'There is another shore, you know, upon the other side.
The further off from England the nearer is to France –
Then turn not pale, beloved snail, but come and join the
    dance.
Will you, won't you, will you, won't you, will you join the
    dance?
Will you, won't you, will you, won't you, won't you join the
    dance?'

The Tyger

William Blake
(1757–1827)

William Blake claimed to have seen many magnificent visions during his lifetime. When he was eight, he saw a tree full of angels with wings decorating the branches like stars. He drew pictures of these religious revelations and wrote about them in his poetry.

This poem is full of words that will make you think of heat – 'burning', 'fire', 'furnace'. Do they remind you of how a tiger's markings look like flames?

★★★

Tyger Tyger, burning bright,
In the forests of the night:
What immortal hand or eye,
Could frame thy fearful symmetry?

In what distant deeps or skies
Burnt the fire of thine eyes!
On what wings dare he aspire?
What the hand, dare sieze the fire?

And what shoulder, and what art,
Could twist the sinews of thy heart?
And when thy heart began to beat,
What dread hand? and what dread feet?

What the hammer? what the chain,
In what furnace was thy brain?
What the anvil? what dread grasp,
Dare its deadly terrors clasp?

When the stars threw down their spears
And water'd heaven with their tears:
Did he smile his work to see?
Did he who made the Lamb make thee?

Tyger, Tyger burning bright,
In the forests of the night:
What immortal hand or eye,
Dare frame thy fearful symmetry?

The Duck and the Kangaroo

Edward Lear
(1812–1888)

Said the Duck to the Kangaroo,
   'Good gracious! how you hop!
Over the fields and the water too,
   As if you never would stop!
My life is a bore in this nasty pond,
And I long to go out in the world beyond!
    I wish I could hop like you!'
    Said the Duck to the Kangaroo.

'Please give me a ride on your back!'
    Said the Duck to the Kangaroo.
'I would sit quite still, and say nothing but "Quack,"
    The whole of the long day through!
And we'd go to the Dee, and the Jelly Bo Lee,
Over the land, and over the sea; –
    Please take me a ride! O do!'
    Said the Duck to the Kangaroo.

Said the Kangaroo to the Duck,
    'This requires some little reflection;
Perhaps on the whole it might bring me luck,
    And there seems but one objection,
Which is, if you'll let me speak so bold,

Your feet are unpleasantly wet and cold,
  And would probably give me the roo-
  Matiz!' said the Kangaroo.

Said the Duck, 'As I sate on the rocks,
  I have thought over that completely,
And I bought four pairs of worsted socks
  Which fit my web-feet neatly.
And to keep out the cold I've bought a cloak,
And every day a cigar I'll smoke,
  All to follow my own dear true
  Love of a Kangaroo!'

Said the Kangaroo, 'I'm ready!
  All in the moonlight pale;
But to balance me well, dear Duck, sit steady!
  And quite at the end of my tail!'
So away they went with a hop and a bound,
And they hopped the whole world three times round;
  And who so happy, – O who,
  As the Duck and the Kangaroo?

The Donkey

G K Chesterton
(1874–1936)

You might be used to seeing pictures of donkeys on Christmas cards, looking cute in a nativity scene. Look again – G K Chesterton's donkey is a bit different. He's a scary creature with a 'monstrous head'. He's forgotten and overlooked, but is that because he's really hideous or because he isn't treated properly? The poem asks you to think twice before you make a judgement. What other animals do you think of as 'ugly'? Could you look at them differently too?

★★★

When fishes flew and forests walked
    And figs grew upon thorn,
Some moment when the moon was blood
    Then surely I was born.

With monstrous head and sickening cry
    And ears like errant wings,
The devil's walking parody
    On all four-footed things.

The tattered outlaw of the earth,
    Of ancient crooked will;
Starve, scourge, deride me: I am dumb,
    I keep my secret still.

Fools! For I also had my hour;
    One far fierce hour and sweet:
There was a shout about my ears,
    And palms before my feet.

The Fish

Elizabeth Bishop
(1911–1979)

I caught a tremendous fish
and held him beside the boat
half out of water, with my hook
fast in a corner of his mouth.
He didn't fight.
He hadn't fought at all.
He hung a grunting weight,
battered and venerable
and homely. Here and there
his brown skin hung in strips
like ancient wallpaper,
and its pattern of darker brown
was like wallpaper:
shapes like full-blown roses
stained and lost through age.
He was speckled with barnacles,
fine rosettes of lime,
and infested
with tiny white sea-lice,
and underneath two or three
rags of green weed hung down.
While his gills were breathing in
the terrible oxygen
– the frightening gills,
fresh and crisp with blood,

that can cut so badly –
I thought of the coarse white flesh
packed in like feathers,
the big bones and the little bones,
the dramatic reds and blacks
of his shiny entrails,
and the pink swim-bladder
like a big peony.
I looked into his eyes
which were far larger than mine
but shallower, and yellowed,
the irises backed and packed
with tarnished tinfoil
seen through the lenses
of old scratched isinglass.
They shifted a little, but not
to return my stare.
– It was more like the tipping
of an object toward the light.
I admired his sullen face,
the mechanism of his jaw,
and then I saw
that from his lower lip
– if you could call it a lip –
grim, wet, and weaponlike,
hung five old pieces of fish-line,
or four and a wire leader
with the swivel still attached,
with all their five big hooks
grown firmly in his mouth.

A green line, frayed at the end
where he broke it, two heavier lines,
and a fine black thread
still crimped from the strain and snap
when it broke and he got away.
Like medals with their ribbons
frayed and wavering,
a five-haired beard of wisdom
trailing from his aching jaw.
I stared and stared
and victory filled up
the little rented boat,
from the pool of bilge
where oil had spread a rainbow
around the rusted engine
to the bailer rusted orange,
the sun-cracked thwarts,
the oarlocks on their strings,
the gunnels – until everything
was rainbow, rainbow, rainbow!
And I let the fish go.

The Spider and the Fly

Mary Howitt
(1799–1888)

Would you walk into a spider's parlour? Maybe not if you were a fly! In this poem, a very cunning spider uses his wits to entice a fly to do just that. He sounds friendly, but it's really a trap. The rhymes at the end of the poem's lines sound a bit sing song, lulling you into a false sense of security, just like the poor fly.

★★★

'Will you walk into my parlour?' said the Spider to the Fly,
''Tis the prettiest little parlour that ever you did spy;
The way into my parlour is up a winding stair,
And I have many curious things to show you when you are
    there.'
'Oh no, no,' said the Fly, 'to ask me is in vain;
For who goes up your winding stair can ne'er come down
    again.'

'I'm sure you must be weary, dear, with soaring up so high;
Will you rest upon my little bed?' said the Spider to the Fly.
'There are pretty curtains drawn around; the sheets are fine
    and thin;
And if you like to rest awhile, I'll snugly tuck you in!'
'Oh no, no,' said the little Fly, 'for I've often heard it said,
They never, never wake again, who sleep upon your bed!'

Said the cunning Spider to the Fly, 'Dear friend what can I do,
To prove the warm affection I've always felt for you?
I have within my pantry, good store of all that's nice;
I'm sure you're very welcome – will you please to take a slice?'
'Oh no, no,' said the little Fly, 'kind sir, that cannot be,
I've heard what's in your pantry, and I do not wish to see!'

'Sweet creature!' said the Spider, 'you're witty and you're wise;
How handsome are your gauzy wings, how brilliant are
    your eyes!
I have a little looking-glass upon my parlour shelf;
If you'll step in a moment, dear, you shall behold yourself.'
'I thank you, gentle sir,' she said, 'for what you're pleased to say;
And bidding you good morning now, I'll call another day.'

The Spider turned him round about, and went into his den,
For well he knew the silly Fly would soon come back again;
So he wove a subtle web, in a little corner sly,
And set his table ready, to dine upon the Fly.
Then he came out to his door again, and merrily did sing,
'Come hither, hither, pretty Fly, with the pearl and silver wing;
Your robes are green and purple, there's a crest upon your head;
Your eyes are like the diamond bright, but mine are dull as lead.'

Alas, alas! How very soon this silly little Fly,
Hearing his wily, flattering words, came slowly flitting by;
With buzzing wings she hung aloft, then near and nearer drew,
Thinking only of her brilliant eyes, and green and purple hue;
Thinking only of her crested head – poor foolish thing! At last,
Up jumped the cunning Spider, and fiercely held her fast.

He dragged her up his winding stair, into his dismal den
Within his little parlour – but she ne'er came out again!

And now, dear little children, who may this story read,
To idle, silly, flattering words, I pray you ne'er give heed:
Unto an evil counsellor close heart, and ear, and eye,
And take a lesson from this tale, of the Spider and the Fly.

Death of a Naturalist

Seamus Heaney
(1939–2013)

All year the flax-dam festered in the heart
Of the townland; green and heavy headed
Flax had rotted there, weighted down by huge sods.
Daily it sweltered in the punishing sun.
Bubbles gargled delicately, bluebottles
Wove a strong gauze of sound around the smell.
There were dragon-flies, spotted butterflies,
But best of all was the warm thick slobber
Of frogspawn that grew like clotted water
In the shade of the banks. Here, every spring
I would fill jampotfuls of the jellied
Specks to range on window-sills at home,
On shelves at school, and wait and watch until
The fattening dots burst into nimble-
Swimming tadpoles. Miss Walls would tell us how
The daddy frog was called a bullfrog
And how he croaked and how the mammy frog
Laid hundreds of little eggs and this was
Frogspawn. You could tell the weather by frogs too
For they were yellow in the sun and brown
In rain.

Then one hot day when fields were rank
With cowdung in the grass the angry frogs
Invaded the flax-dam; I ducked through hedges

To a coarse croaking that I had not heard
Before. The air was thick with a bass chorus.
Right down the dam gross-bellied frogs were cocked
On sods; their loose necks pulsed like sails. Some hopped:
The slap and plop were obscene threats. Some sat
Poised like mud grenades, their blunt heads farting.
I sickened, turned, and ran. The great slime kings
Were gathered there for vengeance and I knew
That if I dipped my hand the spawn would clutch it.

Poor Old Lady

Anonymous

Poor old lady, she swallowed a fly.
I don't know why she swallowed a fly.
Poor old lady, I think she'll die.

Poor old lady, she swallowed a spider.
It squirmed and wriggled and turned inside her.
She swallowed the spider to catch the fly.
I don't know why she swallowed a fly.
Poor old lady, I think she'll die.

Poor old lady, she swallowed a bird.
How absurd! She swallowed a bird.
She swallowed the bird to catch the spider,
She swallowed the spider to catch the fly,
I don't know why she swallowed a fly.
Poor old lady, I think she'll die.

Poor old lady, she swallowed a cat.
Think of that! She swallowed a cat.
She swallowed the cat to catch the bird.
She swallowed the bird to catch the spider.
She swallowed the spider to catch the fly,
I don't know why she swallowed a fly.
Poor old lady, I think she'll die.

Poor old lady, she swallowed a dog.
She went the whole hog when she swallowed the dog.
She swallowed the dog to catch the cat,
She swallowed the cat to catch the bird,
She swallowed the bird to catch the spider.
She swallowed the spider to catch the fly,
I don't know why she swallowed a fly.
Poor old lady, I think she'll die.

Poor old lady, she swallowed a cow.
I don't know how she swallowed a cow.
She swallowed the cow to catch the dog,
She swallowed the dog to catch the cat,
She swallowed the cat to catch the bird,
She swallowed the bird to catch the spider,
She swallowed the spider to catch the fly,
I don't know why she swallowed a fly.
Poor old lady, I think she'll die.

Poor old lady, she swallowed a horse.
She died, of course.

The Panther

Rainer Maria Rilke
Translated by Stephen Mitchell
(1875–1926)

The panther in Rilke's poem is trapped behind bars. In the wild, he'd
be a fierce and proud creature, but held in captivity, he's powerless.
What do you think would happen if he escaped? Rilke describes the
panther's eyes as being like curtains – what does that tell you about
how he sees the world? Is he a part of it or is he separate?

★★★

In the Jardin des Plantes, Paris

His vision, from the constantly passing bars,
has grown so weary that it cannot hold
anything else. It seems to him there are
a thousand bars; and behind the bars, no world.

As he paces in cramped circles, over and over,
the movement of his powerful soft strides
is like a ritual dance around a centre
in which a mighty will stands paralyzed.

Only at times, the curtain of the pupils
lifts, quietly –. An image enters in,
rushes down through the tensed, arrested muscles,
plunges into the heart and is gone.

Hurt No Living Thing

Christina Rossetti
(1830–1894)

Hurt no living thing:
    Ladybird, nor butterfly,
Nor moth with dusty wing,
    Nor cricket chirping cheerily,
Nor grasshopper so light of leap,
    Nor dancing gnat, nor beetle fat,
Nor harmless worms that creep.

The Crocodile

Lewis Carroll
(1832–1898)

How doth the little crocodile
    Improve his shining tail,
And pour the waters of the Nile
    On every golden scale!

How cheerfully he seems to grin,
    How neatly spreads his claws,
And welcomes little fishes in
    With gently smiling jaws!

Nature and
the Seasons

Tall Nettles

Edward Thomas
(1878–1917)

Edward Thomas was killed in the First World War, but unlike some of
the other war poets you will find in this book, he writes more about
nature than he does about battles. 'Tall Nettles' may be set in a small
corner of a farmyard, but it describes the big effects that the things you
see around you can have on you, and how they might make you see the
world differently. What do you see in the corners of your own garden?

★★★

Tall nettles cover up, as they have done
These many springs, the rusty harrow, the plough
Long worn out, and the roller made of stone:
Only the elm butt tops the nettles now.

This corner of the farmyard I like most:
As well as any bloom upon a flower
I like the dust on the nettles, never lost
Except to prove the sweetness of a shower.

No!

Thomas Hood
(1799–1845)

No sun – no moon!
No morn – no noon!
No dawn – no dusk – no proper time of day –
No sky – no earthly view –
No distance looking blue –
No road – no street – no 't'other side this way' –
No end to any Row –
No indications where the Crescents go –
No top to any steeple –
No recognitions of familiar people –
No courtesies for showing 'em –
No knowing 'em!
No travelling at all – no locomotion –
No inkling of the way – no notion –
'No go' by land or ocean –
No mail – no post –
No news from any foreign coast –
No Park, no Ring, no afternoon gentility –
No company – no nobility –
No warmth, no cheerfulness, no healthful ease,
No comfortable feel in any member –
No shade, no shine, no butterflies, no bees,
No fruits, no flowers, no leaves, no birds –
November!

Weathers

Thomas Hardy
(1840–1928)

Thomas Hardy is best known for his novels, but he also wrote poetry, and claimed that verse was his first love.

In this poem, he celebrates both good and bad weather, comparing himself to other things in the natural world (birds, plants and meadows) and how they respond to weather.

★★★

This is the weather the cuckoo likes,
    And so do I;
When showers betumble the chestnut spikes,
    And nestlings fly;
And the little brown nightingale bills his best,
And they sit outside at 'The Traveller's Rest',
And maids come forth sprig-muslin drest,
And citizens dream of the south and west,
    And so do I.

This is the weather the shepherd shuns,
    And so do I;
When beeches drip in browns and duns,
    And thresh and ply;

And hill-hid tides throb, throe on throe,
And meadow rivulets overflow,
And drops on gate bars hang in a row,
And rooks in families homeward go,
    And so do I.

I Wandered Lonely as a Cloud

William Wordsworth
(1770–1850)

Wordsworth lived in the Lake District and this poem was inspired by
a walk that he took with his sister, Dorothy. Dorothy described some
daffodils in her journal and Wordsworth had a quick read to get some
inspiration for this poem. I wonder if she gave him permission to do this
or if he craftily sneaked a peak when she wasn't looking?

The language Wordsworth uses in this poem is very light and airy
– words like 'floats', 'fluttering', 'twinkle', 'sprightly'. How do these
words make you feel? It's as if Wordsworth wants us to fly and hover
over the daffodils to get a proper look at them.

★★★

I wandered lonely as a cloud
That floats on high o'er vales and hills,
When all at once I saw a crowd,
A host, of golden daffodils;
Beside the lake, beneath the trees,
Fluttering and dancing in the breeze.

Continuous as the stars that shine
And twinkle on the milky way,
They stretched in never-ending line
Along the margin of a bay:
Ten thousand saw I at a glance,

Tossing their heads in sprightly dance.

The waves beside them danced; but they
Out-did the sparkling waves in glee:
A poet could not but be gay,
In such a jocund company:
I gazed – and gazed – but little thought
What wealth the show to me had brought:

For oft, when on my couch I lie
In vacant or in pensive mood,
They flash upon that inward eye
Which is the bliss of solitude;
And then my heart with pleasure fills,
And dances with the daffodils.

May

Christina Rossetti
(1830–1894)

I cannot tell you how it was;
But this I know: it came to pass
Upon a bright and breezy day
When May was young; ah pleasant May!
As yet the poppies were not born
Between the blades of tender corn;
The last eggs had not hatched as yet,
Nor any bird forgone its mate.

I cannot tell you what it was;
But this I know: it did but pass.
It passed away with sunny May,
With all sweet things it passed away,
And left me old, and cold, and grey.

Afternoon on a Hill

Edna St Vincent Millay
(1892–1950)

I will be the gladdest thing
    Under the sun!
I will touch a hundred flowers
    And not pick one.

I will look at cliffs and clouds
    With quiet eyes,
Watch the wind bow down the grass,
    And the grass rise.

And when lights begin to show
    Up from the town,
I will mark which must be mine,
    And then start down!

To Autumn

John Keats
(1795–1821)

This is a poem that John Keats wrote after a walk one night. What things do you see in autumn if you walk out of your front door? Keats saw trees heavy with fruit, mist, poppies and late flowers for the bees. In spring, new life begins but in autumn things begin to fade. The poem shows that autumn is a lovely season even though it is an ending rather than a beginning.

★★★

Season of mists and mellow fruitfulness,
    Close bosom-friend of the maturing sun,
Conspiring with him how to load and bless
    With fruit the vines that round the thatch-eaves run;
To bend with apples the mossed cottage-trees,
    And fill all fruit with ripeness to the core;
      To swell the gourd, and plump the hazel shells
    With a sweet kernel; to set budding more,
And still more, later flowers for the bees,
Until they think warm days will never cease,
    For Summer has o'er-brimmed their clammy cells.

Who hath not seen thee oft amid thy store?
    Sometimes whoever seeks abroad may find
Thee sitting careless on a granary floor,
    Thy hair soft-lifted by the winnowing wind;

Or on a half-reaped furrow sound asleep,
    Drowsed with the fume of poppies, while thy hook
        Spares the next swath and all its twinèd flowers;
And sometimes like a gleaner thou dost keep
    Steady thy laden head across a brook;
    Or by a cyder-press, with patient look,
        Thou watchest the last oozings hours by hours.

Where are the songs of Spring? Ay, where are they?
    Think not of them, thou hast thy music too –
While barrèd clouds bloom the soft-dying day,
    And touch the stubble-plains with rosy hue:
Then in a wailful choir the small gnats mourn
    Among the river sallows, borne aloft
        Or sinking as the light wind lives or dies;
And full-grown lambs loud bleat from hilly bourn;
    Hedge-crickets sing; and now with treble soft
    The red-breast whistles from a garden-croft;
        And gathering swallows twitter in the skies.

From *As You Like It*

William Shakespeare
(1564–1616)

Under the greenwood tree,
   Who loves to lie with me,
And turn his merry note
   Unto the sweet bird's throat,
Come hither, come hither, come hither.
   Here shall he see
   No enemy,
But winter and rough weather.

...

Who doth ambition shun,
   And loves to live i'th' sun,
Seeking the food he eats,
   And pleas'd with what he gets,
Come hither, come hither, come hither.
   Here shall he see
   No enemy,
But winter and rough weather.

Bed in Summer

Robert Louis Stevenson
(1850–1894)

In winter I get up at night
And dress by yellow candle-light.
In summer, quite the other way,
I have to go to bed by day.

I have to go to bed and see
The birds still hopping on the tree,
Or hear the grown-up people's feet
Still going past me in the street.

And does it not seem hard to you,
When all the sky is clear and blue,
And I should like so much to play,
To have to go to bed by day?

Pleasant Sounds

John Clare
(1793–1864)

John Clare was known as the 'Northamptonshire Peasant Poet' and often preferred to write in something called dialect – the words and pronunciations used by people in one area, but not in the rest of the country. What words do you use that other people might not?

Sadly, Clare spent the last part of his life in hospitals called asylums. He famously escaped from one asylum in Essex and decided to walk all the way back to the place where he was born.

★★★

The rustling of leaves under the feet in woods and under
    hedges;
The crumping of cat-ice and snow down wood-rides, narrow
    lanes, and every street causeway;
Rustling through a wood or rather rushing, while the wind
    halloos in the oak-top like thunder;
The rustle of birds' wings startled from their nests or flying
    unseen into the bushes;
The whizzing of larger birds overhead in a wood, such as
    crows, puddocks, buzzards;
The trample of robins and wood-larks on the brown leaves,
    and the patter of squirrels on the green moss;
The fall of an acorn on the ground, the pattering of nuts on
    the hazel branches as they fall from ripeness;

The flirt of the ground lark's wing from the stubbles – how
sweet such pictures on dewy mornings, when the
dew flashes from its brown feathers!

The Pleiades

Amy Lowell
(1874–1925)

By day you cannot see the sky
For it is up so very high.
You look and look, but it's so blue
That you can never see right through.

But when night comes it is quite plain,
And all the stars are there again.
They seem just like old friends to me,
I've known them all my life you see.

There is the dipper first, and there
Is Cassiopeia in her chair,
Orion's belt, the Milky Way,
And lots I know but cannot say.

One group looks like a swarm of bees,
Papa says they're the Pleiades;
But I think they must be the toy
Of some nice little angel boy.

Perhaps his jackstones which to-day
He has forgot to put away,
And left them lying on the sky
Where he will find them bye and bye.

I wish he'd come and play with me.
We'd have such fun, for it would be
A most unusual thing for boys
To feel that they had stars for toys!

Monsters,
Beasts and Fairies

The Kraken

Alfred, Lord Tennyson
(1809–1892)

Below the thunders of the upper deep,
Far, far beneath in the abysmal sea,
His ancient, dreamless, uninvaded sleep
The Kraken sleepeth: faintest sunlights flee
About his shadowy sides; above him swell
Huge sponges of millennial growth and height;
And far away into the sickly light,
From many a wondrous grot and secret cell
Unnumber'd and enormous polypi
Winnow with giant arms the slumbering green.
There hath he lain for ages, and will lie
Battening upon huge sea-worms in his sleep,
Until the latter fire shall heat the deep;
Then once by man and angels to be seen,
In roaring he shall rise and on the surface die.

Jabberwocky

Lewis Carroll
(1832–1898)

'Twas brillig, and the slithy toves
    Did gyre and gimble in the wabe:
All mimsy were the borogoves,
    And the mome raths outgrabe.

'Beware the Jabberwock, my son!
    The jaws that bite, the claws that catch!
Beware the Jubjub bird, and shun
    The frumious Bandersnatch!'

He took his vorpal sword in hand:
    Long time the manxome foe he sought –
So rested he by the Tumtum tree,
    And stood awhile in thought.

And, as in uffish thought he stood,
    The Jabberwock, with eyes of flame,
Came whiffling through the tulgey wood,
    And burbled as it came!

One, two! One, two! And through and through
    The vorpal blade went snicker-snack!
He left it dead, and with its head
    He went galumphing back.

'And hast thou slain the Jabberwock?
　　Come to my arms, my beamish boy!
Oh frabjous day! Callooh! Callay!'
　　He chortled in his joy.

'Twas brillig, and the slithy toves
　　Did gyre and gimble in the wabe:
All mimsy were the borogoves,
　　And the mome raths outgrabe.

From *The Tempest*

William Shakespeare
(1564–1616)

The action in this play by Shakespeare takes place on a remote island where a magician called Prospero, who is also an exiled duke, wants to restore his heir (Miranda) to the throne. He conjures up a storm to bring his brother and others who plotted against him to the island. This extract is spoken by a strange, half-human creature called Caliban. Caliban is ruthless and vicious (he is the son of a witch after all) but Shakespeare sometimes gives him some lovely, descriptive speeches to show off the creature's softer side.

★★★

Be not afeard; the isle is full of noises,
Sounds, and sweet airs, that give delight and hurt not.
Sometimes a thousand twangling instruments
Will hum about mine ears, and sometime voices,
That, if I then had waked after long sleep,
Will make me sleep again: and then, in dreaming,
The clouds methought would open, and show riches
Ready to drop upon me; that, when I waked,
I cried to dream again.

From *A Midsummer Night's Dream*

William Shakespeare
(1564–1616)

Shakespeare's most famous comedy is set in a magical wood, just outside Athens, where lots of fairies live (including the fairy king and queen). This, the final speech in the play, is spoken by a mischievous sprite called Puck. At one point he transforms a man's head into the head of a donkey!

***

If we shadows have offended,
Think but this, and all is mended,
That you have but slumber'd here
While these visions did appear.
And this weak and idle theme,
No more yielding but a dream,
Gentles, do not reprehend:
If you pardon, we will mend:
And, as I am an honest Puck,
If we have unearned luck
Now to 'scape the serpent's tongue,
We will make amends ere long;
Else the Puck a liar call;
So, good night unto you all.
Give me your hands, if we be friends,
And Robin shall restore amends.

In the Forest

Oscar Wilde
(1854–1900)

Out of the mid-wood's twilight
    Into the meadow's dawn,
Ivory-limbed and brown-eyed,
    Flashes my Faun!

He skips through the copses singing,
    And his shadow dances along,
And I know not which I should follow,
    Shadow or song!

O Hunter, snare me his shadow!
    O Nightingale, catch me his strain!
Else moonstruck with music and madness
    I track him in vain!

The Fairies

William Allingham
(1824–1889)

Up the airy mountain,
    Down the rushy glen,
We daren't go a-hunting,
    For fear of little men;
Wee folk, good folk,
    Trooping all together;
Green jacket, red cap,
    And white owl's feather!

Down along the rocky shore
    Some make their home,
They live on crispy pancakes
    Of yellow tide-foam;
Some in the reeds
    Of the black mountain-lake,
With frogs for their watch-dogs,
    All night awake.

High on the hill-top
    The old King sits;
He is now so old and grey,
    He's nigh lost his wits.
With a bridge of white mist
    Columbkill he crosses,

On his stately journeys
　　From Slieveleague to Rosses;
Or going up with music,
　　On cold starry nights,
To sup with the Queen
　　Of the gay Northern Lights.

They stole little Bridget
　　For seven years long;
When she came down again
　　Her friends were all gone.
They took her lightly back
　　Between the night and morrow;
They thought that she was fast asleep,
　　But she was dead with sorrow.
They have kept her ever since
　　Deep within the lake,
On a bed of flag-leaves,
　　Watching till she wake.

By the craggy hillside,
　　Through the mosses bare,
They have planted thorn-trees
　　For pleasure here and there.
Is any man so daring
　　As dig them up in spite?
He shall find the thornies set
　　In his bed at night.

Up the airy mountain,
    Down the rushy glen,
We daren't go a-hunting,
    For fear of little men;
Wee folk, good folk,
    Trooping all together;
Green jacket, red cap,
    And white owl's feather!

Goblin Market (an extract)

Christina Rossetti
(1830–1894)

Christina Rossetti was one of the most famous female poets of her time – a time when famous female writers were very rare.

In 'Goblin Market', two sisters get into trouble after one of them (Laura) eats bewitched fruit sold by goblin merchants. When Laura is unable to get any more of the goblin fruit, she falls ill and her sister Lizzie is afraid she will die. Lizzie tries to buy more fruit from the goblins in the hope she can save her sister, but they angrily pelt her with fruit, drenching her clothes with the juices. Clever Lizzie hopes that her sister might still be cured by drinking the juice from her body and returns home, where, eventually, Laura returns to health after tasting some of the fruit juice. The two live to warn their own children against the trickery of the goblins and their forbidden fruit.

This poem is written in very short lines and a sing-song rhyme – you can almost hear the goblins calling out to Lizzie and Laura from the page.

★★★

Morning and evening
Maids heard the goblins cry:
'Come buy our orchard fruits,
Come buy, come buy:
Apples and quinces,

Lemons and oranges,
Plump unpecked cherries,
Melons and raspberries,
Bloom-down-cheeked peaches,
Swart-headed mulberries,
Wild free-born cranberries,
Crab-apples, dewberries,
Pine-apples, blackberries,
Apricots, strawberries; –
All ripe together
In summer weather, –
Morns that pass by,
Fair eves that fly;
Come buy, come buy:
Our grapes fresh from the vine,
Pomegranates full and fine,
Dates and sharp bullaces,
Rare pears and greengages,
Damsons and bilberries,
Taste them and try:
Currants and gooseberries,
Bright-fire-like barberries,
Figs to fill your mouth,
Citrons from the South,
Sweet to tongue and sound to eye;
Come buy, come buy.'

Evening by evening
Among the brookside rushes,
Laura bowed her head to hear,

Lizzie veiled her blushes:
Crouching close together
In the cooling weather,
With clasping arms and cautioning lips,
With tingling cheeks and finger tips.
'Lie close,' Laura said,
Pricking up her golden head:
'We must not look at goblin men,
We must not buy their fruits:
Who knows upon what soil they fed
Their hungry thirsty roots?'
'Come buy,' call the goblins
Hobbling down the glen.
'Oh,' cried Lizzie, 'Laura, Laura,
You should not peep at goblin men.'
Lizzie covered up her eyes,
Covered close lest they should look;
Laura reared her glossy head,
And whispered like the restless brook:
'Look, Lizzie, look, Lizzie,
Down the glen tramp little men.
One hauls a basket,
One bears a plate,
One lugs a golden dish
Of many pounds weight.
How fair the vine must grow
Whose grapes are so luscious;
How warm the wind must blow
Thro' those fruit bushes.'
'No,' said Lizzie, 'No, no, no;

Their offers should not charm us,
Their evil gifts would harm us.'
She thrust a dimpled finger
In each ear, shut eyes and ran:
Curious Laura chose to linger
Wondering at each merchant man.
One had a cat's face,
One whisked a tail,
One tramped at a rat's pace,
One crawled like a snail,
One like a wombat prowled obtuse and furry,
One like a ratel tumbled hurry skurry.
She heard a voice like voice of doves
Cooing all together:
They sounded kind and full of loves
In the pleasant weather.

From *Macbeth*

William Shakespeare
(1564–1616)

William Shakespeare is England's most famous writer, poet, playwright and actor. His plays have been translated into every living language and performed more than any other playwright in the world. He produced just under 40 plays in his lifetime, and this extract is taken from one called *Macbeth*.

★★★

FIRST WITCH
Round about the cauldron go –
In the poisoned entrails throw.
Toad, that under cold stone
Days and nights has thirty-one,
Sweltered venom sleeping got:
Boil thou first i'th' charmèd pot.

ALL
Double, double, toil and trouble,
Fire burn, and cauldron bubble.

SECOND WITCH
Fillet of a fenny snake
In the cauldron boil and bake;
Eye of newt, and toe of frog,
Wool of bat, and tongue of dog;

Adder's fork, and blind-worm's sting,
Lizard's leg, and howlet's wing:
For a charm of powerful trouble,
Like a hell-broth, boil and bubble.

ALL
Double, double, toil and trouble,
Fire burn and cauldron bubble.

THIRD WITCH
Scale of dragon, tooth of wolf,
Witch's mummy, maw and gulf
Of the ravined salt-sea shark;
Root of hemlock, digged i'th' dark;
Liver of blaspheming Jew,
Gall of goat, and slips of yew
Slivered in the moon's eclipse;
Nose of Turk, and Tartar's lips;
Finger of birth-strangled babe
Ditch-delivered by a drab:
Make the gruel thick and slab;
Add thereto a tiger's chawdron,
For th' ingredience of our cauldron.

ALL
Double, double, toil and trouble,
Fire burn and cauldron bubble.

Humour
and
Nonsense

There Was an Old Man
with a Beard

Edward Lear
(1812–1888)

There was an Old Man with a beard,
Who said, 'It is just as I feared! –
Two Owls and a Hen,
Four Larks and a Wren,
Have all built their nests in my beard.'

Cautionary Playground Rhyme

Ian McMillan
(1956–)

Natasha Green
Natasha Green
stuck her head in a washing machine

Washing Machine
Washing Machine
round and round Natasha Green

Natasha Green
Natasha Green
cleanest girl I've ever seen

Ever Seen
Ever Seen
a girl with her head in a washing machine?

Washing Machine
Washing Machine
last home of Natasha Green

Natasha Green
Natasha Green
washed away in a white machine

White Machine
White Machine
soaped to death Natasha Green

Natasha Green
Natasha Green
cleanest ghost I've ever seen!

MORAL:

Washing machines are for knickers and blouses
Washing machines are for jumpers and trousers
Keep your head out of the washing machine
or you'll end up as spotless as little Miss Green.

The Dong with a Luminous Nose

Edward Lear
(1812–1888)

When awful darkness and silence reign
Over the great Gromboolian plain,
    Through the long, long wintry nights; –
When the angry breakers roar
As they beat on the rocky shore; –
    When Storm-clouds brood on the towering heights
Of the Hills of the Chankly Bore: –

Then, through the vast and gloomy dark,
There moves what seems a fiery spark,
        A lonely spark with silvery rays
        Piercing the coal-black night, –
        A meteor strange and bright: –
    Hither and thither the vision strays,
        A single lurid light.

Slowly it wanders, – pauses, – creeps, –
Anon it sparkles, – flashes and leaps;
And ever as onward it gleaming goes
A light on the Bong-tree stems it throws.
And those who watch at that midnight hour
From Hall or Terrace, or lofty Tower,
Cry, as the wild light passes along, –
        'The Dong! – the Dong!
    The wandering Dong through the forest goes!

The Dong! the Dong!
The Dong with a luminous Nose!'

Long years ago
The Dong was happy and gay,
Till he fell in love with a Jumbly Girl
Who came to those shores one day.
For the Jumblies came in a Sieve, they did, –
Landing at eve near the Zemmery Fidd
Where the Oblong Oysters grow,
And the rocks are smooth and grey.
And all the woods and the valleys rang
With the Chorus they daily and nightly sang, –
'Far and few, far and few,
Are the lands where the Jumblies live;
Their heads are green, and their hands are blue
And they went to sea in a Sieve.'

Happily, happily passed those days!
While the cheerful Jumblies staid;
They danced in circlets all night long,
To the plaintive pipe of the lively Dong,
In moonlight, shine, or shade.
For day and night he was always there
By the side of the Jumbly Girl so fair,
With her sky-blue hands, and her sea-green hair.
Till the morning came of that hateful day
When the Jumblies sailed in their Sieve away,
And the Dong was left on the cruel shore
Gazing – gazing for evermore, –

Ever keeping his weary eyes on
That pea-green sail on the far horizon, –
Singing the Jumbly Chorus still
As he sate all day on the grassy hill, –
> *'Far and few, far and few,*
> *Are the lands where the Jumblies live;*
> *Their heads are green, and their hands are blue*
> *And they went to sea in a Sieve.'*

But when the sun was low in the West,
> The Dong arose and said; –
'What little sense I once possessed
> Has quite gone out of my head!'
And since that day he wanders still
By lake and forest, marsh and hill,
Singing – 'O somewhere, in valley or plain
Might I find my Jumbly Girl again!
For ever I'll seek by lake and shore
Till I find my Jumbly Girl once more!'

> Playing a pipe with silvery squeaks,
> Since then his Jumbly Girl he seeks,
> And because by night he could not see,
> He gathered the bark of the Twangum Tree
> > On the flowery plain that grows.
> > And he wove him a wondrous Nose, –
> A Nose as strange as a Nose could be!
Of vast proportions and painted red,
And tied with cords to the back of his head.
> – In a hollow rounded space it ended

With a luminous lamp within suspended,
    All fenced about
    With a bandage stout
    To prevent the wind from blowing it out; –
And with holes all round to send the light,
In gleaming rays on the dismal night.

And now each night, and all night long,
Over those plains still roams the Dong;
And above the wail of the Chimp and Snipe
You may hear the squeak of his plaintive pipe
    While ever he seeks, but seeks in vain
To meet with his Jumbly Girl again;
Lonely and wild – all night he goes, –
The Dong with a luminous Nose!
And all who watch at the midnight hour,
From Hall or Terrace, or lofty Tower,
Cry, as they trace the Meteor bright,
Moving along through the dreary night, –
    'This is the hour when forth he goes,
    The Dong with the luminous Nose!
    Yonder – over the plain he goes;
        He goes!
        He goes;
    The Dong with the luminous Nose!'

The Uncertainty of the Poet

Wendy Cope
(1945–)

Wendy Cope is best known for her humorous verse. This poem is
based around two sentences, combining poets and bananas to
surprising effect. How many ways could you rearrange a group of ten
words to get different meanings out of them?

★★★

I am a poet.
I am very fond of bananas.

I am bananas.
I am very fond of a poet.

I am a poet of bananas.
I am very fond.

A fond poet of 'I am, I am' –
Very bananas.

Fond of 'Am I bananas?
Am I?' – a very poet.

Bananas of a poet!
Am I fond? Am I very?

Poet bananas! I am.
I am fond of a 'very'.

I am of very fond bananas.
Am I a poet?

The Akond of Swat

Edward Lear
(1812–1888)

WHO, or why, or which, or what,
    Is the Akond of Swat?

Is he tall or short, or dark or fair?
Does he sit on a stool or a sofa or chair,
      OR SQUAT?
        The Akond of Swat?

Is he wise or foolish, young or old?
Does he drink his soup and his coffee cold,
      OR HOT,
        The Akond of Swat?

Does he sing or whistle, jabber or talk,
And when riding abroad does he gallop or walk,
      OR TROT,
        The Akond of Swat?

Does he wear a turban, a fez or a hat?
Does he sleep on a mattress, a bed, or a mat,
      OR A COT,
        The Akond of Swat?

When he writes a copy in round-hand size,
Does he cross his T's and finish his I's
WITH A DOT,
The Akond of Swat?

Can he write a letter concisely clear
Without a speck or a smudge or a smear
OR BLOT,
The Akond of Swat?

Do his people like him extremely well?
Or do they, whenever they can, rebel,
OR PLOT,
At the Akond of Swat?

If he catches them then, either old or young,
Does he have them chopped in pieces or hung,
OR SHOT,
The Akond of Swat?

Do his people prig in the lanes or park?
Or even at times when days are dark,
GAROTTE?
O the Akond of Swat!

Does he study the wants of his own dominion?
Or doesn't he care for public opinion
A JOT,
The Akond of Swat?

To amuse his mind do the people show him
Pictures, or anyone's last new poem,
   OR WHAT,
    For the Akond of Swat?

At night if he suddenly screams and wakes,
Do they bring him only a few small cakes,
   OR A LOT,
    For the Akond of Swat?

Does he live on turnips, tea, or tripe?
Does he like his shawl to be marked with a stripe,
   OR A DOT,
    The Akond of Swat?

Does he like to lie on his back in a boat
Like the lady who lived in that isle remote,
   SHALOTT,
    The Akond of Swat?

Is he quiet or always making a fuss?
Is his steward a Swiss or a Swede or Russ,
   OR A SCOT,
    The Akond of Swat?

Does he like to sit by the calm blue wave?
Or to sleep and snore in a dark green cave,
   OR A GROTT,
    The Akond of Swat?

Does he drink small beer from a silver jug?
Or a bowl? or a glass? or a cup? or a mug?
    OR A POT,
    The Akond of Swat?

Does he beat his wife with a gold-topped pipe,
When she lets the gooseberries grow too ripe,
    OR ROT,
    The Akond of Swat?

Does he wear a white tie when he dines with friends,
And tie it neat in a bow with ends,
    OR A KNOT,
    The Akond of Swat?

Does he like new cream and hate mince-pies?
When he looks at the sun does he wink his eyes,
    OR NOT,
    The Akond of Swat?

Does he teach his subjects to roast and bake?
Does he sail about on an inland lake,
    IN A YACHT,
    The Akond of Swat?

Some one, or nobody, knows I wot
Who or which or why or what
    Is the Akond of Swat!

The Computer's First Christmas Card

Edwin Morgan
(1920–2010)

```
jollymerry
hollyberry
jollyberry
merryholly
happyjolly
jollyjelly
jellybelly
bellymerry
hollyheppy
jollyMolly
marryJerry
merryHarry
hoppyBarry
heppyJarry
boppyheppy
berryjorry
jorryjolly
moppyjelly
Mollymerry
Jerryjolly
bellyboppy
jorryhoppy
hollymoppy
Barrymerry
Jarryhappy
```

```
happyboppy
boppyjolly
jollymerry
merrymerry
merrymerry
merryChris
ammerryasa
Chrismerry
asMERRYCHR
YSANTHEMUM
```

The Pobble Who Has No Toes

Edward Lear
(1812–1888)

The Pobble who has no toes
Had once as many as we;
When they said, 'Some day you may lose them all;' –
He replied, – 'Fish fiddle de-dee!'
And his Aunt Jobiska made him drink,
Lavender water tinged with pink,
For she said, 'The World in general knows
There's nothing so good for a Pobble's toes!'

The Pobble who has no toes,
Swam across the Bristol Channel;
But before he set out he wrapped his nose,
In a piece of scarlet flannel.
For his Aunt Jobiska said, 'No harm
Can come to his toes if his nose is warm;
And it's perfectly known that a Pobble's toes
Are safe, – provided he minds his nose.'

The Pobble swam fast and well
And when boats or ships came near him
He tinkledy-blinkledy-winkled a bell
So that all the world could hear him.
And all the Sailors and Admirals cried,
When they saw him nearing the further side, –

'He has gone to fish, for his Aunt Jobiska's
Runcible Cat with crimson whiskers!'

But before he touched the shore,
The shore of the Bristol Channel,
A sea-green Porpoise carried away
His wrapper of scarlet flannel.
And when he came to observe his feet
Formerly garnished with toes so neat
His face at once became forlorn
On perceiving that all his toes were gone!

And nobody ever knew
From that dark day to the present,
Whoso had taken the Pobble's toes,
In a manner so far from pleasant.
Whether the shrimps or crawfish grey,
Or crafty Mermaids stole them away –
Nobody knew; and nobody knows
How the Pobble was robbed of his twice five toes!

The Pobble who has no toes
Was placed in a friendly Bark,
And they rowed him back, and carried him up,
To his Aunt Jobiska's Park.
And she made him a feast at his earnest wish
Of eggs and buttercups fried with fish; –
And she said, – 'It's a fact the whole world knows,
That Pobbles are happier without their toes.'

The Mad Gardener's Song

Lewis Carroll
(1832–1898)

He thought he saw an Elephant,
That practised on a fife:
He looked again, and found it was
A letter from his wife.
'At length I realise,' he said,
'The bitterness of Life!'

He thought he saw a Buffalo
Upon the chimney-piece:
He looked again, and found it was
His Sister's Husband's Niece.
'Unless you leave this house,' he said,
'I'll send for the Police!'

He thought he saw a Rattlesnake
That questioned him in Greek:
He looked again, and found it was
The Middle of Next Week.
'The one thing I regret,' he said,
'Is that it cannot speak!'

He thought he saw a Banker's Clerk
Descending from the bus:
He looked again, and found it was
A Hippopotamus

'If this should stay to dine,' he said,
'There won't be much for us!'

He thought he saw a Kangaroo
That worked a coffee-mill:
He looked again, and found it was
A Vegetable-Pill.
'Were I to swallow this,' he said,
'I should be very ill!'

He thought he saw a Coach-and-Four
That stood beside his bed:
He looked again, and found it was
A Bear without a Head.
'Poor thing,' he said, 'poor silly thing!
It's waiting to be fed!'

He thought he saw an Albatross
That fluttered round the lamp:
He looked again, and found it was
A Penny Postage Stamp.
'You'd best be getting home,' he said:
'The nights are very damp!'

He thought he saw a Garden-Door
That opened with a key:
He looked again, and found it was
A Double Rule of Three:
'And all its mystery,' he said,
'Is clear as day to me!'

He thought he saw an Argument
That proved he was the Pope:
He looked again, and found it was
A Bar of Mottled Soap.
'A fact so dread,' he faintly said,
'Extinguishes all hope!'

Love and
Beauty

Valentine

Carol Ann Duffy
(1955–)

Carol Ann Duffy was born in Scotland. In 2009 she was appointed
Poet Laureate, the first woman to hold the position. She often writes
poems from the point of view of famous men's wives or sisters or other
female characters. 'Valentine' describes a present given to a lover
on Valentine's Day, but the gift in Duffy's poem isn't the usual card or
flowers or chocolates … How would you feel if someone gave you an
onion as a present?

★★★

Not a red rose or a satin heart.

I give you an onion.
It is a moon wrapped in brown paper.
It promises light
like the careful undressing of love.

Here.
It will blind you with tears
like a lover.
It will make your reflection
a wobbling photo of grief.

I am trying to be truthful.

Not a cute card or a kissogram.

I give you an onion.
Its fierce kiss will stay on your lips,
possessive and faithful
as we are,
for as long as we are.

Take it.
Its platinum loops shrink to a wedding-ring,
if you like.
Lethal.
Its scent will cling to your fingers,
cling to your knife.

Composed Upon Westminster Bridge, September 3, 1802

William Wordsworth
(1770–1850)

William Wordsworth was a famous 'Romantic' poet – but that doesn't mean he wrote about love – Romantic poets wrote about the natural world and people's emotional responses to it. People sometimes mock the Romantics for being soppy and for writing poems about boring things like vases and rocks, but they produced some of the best poetry the world has to offer.

★★★

Earth has not anything to show more fair:
Dull would he be of soul who could pass by
A sight so touching in its majesty:
This City now doth, like a garment, wear
The beauty of the morning; silent, bare,
Ships, towers, domes, theatres, and temples lie
Open unto the fields, and to the sky;
All bright and glittering in the smokeless air.
Never did sun more beautifully steep
In his first splendour, valley, rock, or hill;
Ne'er saw I, never felt, a calm so deep!
The river glideth at his own sweet will:
Dear God! the very houses seem asleep;
And all that mighty heart is lying still!

Sonnet 73

William Shakespeare
(1564–1616)

That time of year thou mayst in me behold,
When yellow leaves, or none, or few, do hang
Upon those boughs which shake against the cold,
Bare ruin'd choirs, where late the sweet birds sang.
In me thou see'st the twilight of such day,
As after sunset fadeth in the west,
Which by and by black night doth take away,
Death's second self, that seals up all in rest.
In me thou see'st the glowing of such fire,
That on the ashes of his youth doth lie,
As the death-bed whereon it must expire,
Consum'd with that which it was nourish'd by.
    This thou perceiv'st, which makes thy love more strong,
    To love that well, which thou must leave ere long.

The Back Seat of My Mother's Car

Julia Copus
(1969–)

This poem is written in a very unusual form, one which the poet invented
herself. Do you notice anything about how the two verses are written?
Julia calls the form a 'specular' which means 'mirror' in Latin. You might
have noticed how the second half of the poem uses the same lines as
the first, but in the opposite order. The poem describes a child being
driven away from her father after her parents have split up, so the child
might be watching everything that is happening through the mirror in
the car.

★★★

We left before I had time
to comfort you, to tell you that we nearly touched
hands in that vacuous half-dark. I wanted
to stem the burning waters running over me like tiny
rivers down my face and legs, but at the same time I was
    reaching out
for the slit in the window where the sky streamed in,
cold as ether, and I could see your fat mole-fingers grasping
the dusty August air. I pressed my face to the glass;
I was calling to you – Daddy! – as we screeched away into
the distance, my own hand tingling like an amputation.
You were mouthing something I still remember, the noiseless
    words

piercing me like that catgut shriek that flew up, furious as a
    sunset
pouring itself out against the sky. The ensuing silence
was the one clear thing I could decipher –
the roar of the engine drowning your voice,
with the cool slick glass between us.

With the cool slick glass between us,
the roar of the engine drowning, your voice
was the one clear thing I could decipher –
pouring itself out against the sky, the ensuing silence
piercing me like that catgut shriek that flew up, furious as a
    sunset.
You were mouthing something: I still remember the noiseless
    words,
the distance, my own hand tingling like an amputation.
I was calling to you, Daddy, as we screeched away into
the dusty August air. I pressed my face to the glass,
cold as ether, and I could see your fat mole-fingers grasping
for the slit in the window where the sky streamed in
rivers down my face and legs, but at the same time I was
    reaching out
to stem the burning waters running over me like tiny
hands in that vacuous half-dark. I wanted
to comfort you, to tell you that we nearly touched.
We left before I had time.

The Sun Rising

John Donne
(1572–1631)

Busy old fool, unruly Sun,
Why dost thou thus,
Through windows, and through curtains call on us?
Must to thy motions lovers' seasons run?
Saucy pedantic wretch, go chide
Late schoolboys and sour prentices,
Go tell court-huntsmen that the King will ride,
Call country ants to harvest offices;
Love, all alike, no season knows, nor clime,
Nor hours, days, months, which are the rags of time.

Thy beams, so reverend, and strong
Why shouldst thou think?
I could eclipse and cloud them with a wink,
But that I would not lose her sight so long:
If her eyes have not blinded thine,
Look, and tomorrow late, tell me,
Whether both the Indias of spice and mine
Be where thou leftst them, or lie here with me.
Ask for those kings whom thou saw'st yesterday,
And thou shalt hear, All here in one bed lay.

She's all states, and all princes, I,
Nothing else is.
Princes do but play us; compared to this,

All honor's mimic, all wealth alchemy.
>   Thou sun, art half as happy as we,
>   In that the world's contracted thus:
> Thine age asks ease, and since thy duties be
> To warm the world, that's done in warming us.
Shine here to us, and thou art everywhere;
This bed thy center is, these walls, thy sphere.

Tam Lin's Wife

Clare Pollard
(1978–)

Clare Pollard published her first book of poetry when she was just
nineteen years old. In this poem, she draws on the ballad of Tam
Lin, from the Scottish Borders. In the ballad, a man named Tam Lin is
captured by the Queen of the Fairies and has to be rescued by his
true love, Janet. Tam Lin tells Janet the fairies will try to reclaim him for
their own at midnight on Halloween. After the clock strikes the hour,
the fairy folk will ride past Janet. He warns her that he will be turned
into all manner of terrifying forms and finally a burning coal. When this
happens, she must throw him into water, and then finally he will turn
into a man.

★★★

They sat us in a pale and private place,
quietly conveyed the worst –
explained the curse that was your fate
and how for one long, ill-starred night
you'd turn and burn, become all beasts
you could dream up.
I think that I cried out. They said
that if I want to have you
then I have to hold,
to hang on tight and not let go,
and not let go,
until you wake entire again within my arms –

pale skin, dark tufts of hair, long bones –
in crumpled daylight.
And now the sun has sunk, dark taken hold,
and in my hug you jolt
to sudden adder, X-marked, zigzagged, venom-
quick, then rear to brute-necked dog,
as black as forests and spume-jawed.
I tell myself that you are still my love
although I'm wet with blood, and you're a lynx
filthy with fingerprints, clean pink mouth snapping teeth
near heart, my throat.
I keep you caught and don't let go,
and don't let go,
and feel your skull become a bleach December sun,
your eyes hot coals, you burst to blaze: a wicker-man.
You're searing through my fingers,
molten lead.
Dear husband, all those things I prize in you –
your beauty, kindness, laugh –
are stripped off one by one
but even with them gone
my boy stares out from stricken shapes,
and love has no conditions. None.

When You Are Old

William Butler Yeats
(1865–1939)

Yeats' poem addresses a young woman and asks her to imagine she
is old already and remembering her youth. As an old woman, she will
remember how her beauty was admired by many people, but that only
one man loved her for who she really was. This person is the speaker
of the poem and the poem is a reminder that she should not take his
love for granted.

★★★

When you are old and grey and full of sleep,
And nodding by the fire, take down this book,
And slowly read, and dream of the soft look
Your eyes had once, and of their shadows deep;

How many loved your moments of glad grace,
And loved your beauty with love false or true,
But one man loved the pilgrim soul in you,
And loved the sorrows of your changing face;

And bending down beside the glowing bars,
Murmur, a little sadly, how Love fled
And paced upon the mountains overhead
And hid his face amid a crowd of stars.

Hodgepodge
Poems

How to Disappear

Amanda Dalton
(1957–)

Amanda Dalton is a poet and playwright. In this poem, she presents a set of instructions for disappearing. The person in the poem is slowly losing things, starting with easy objects (such as keys and umbrellas) and moving on to things that are more difficult. What things would you least like to lose? What do you think happens at the end of Amanda's poem?

★★★

First rehearse the easy things.
Lose your words in a high wind,
walk in the dark on an unlit road,
observe how other people mislay keys,
their diaries, new umbrellas.
See what it takes to go unnoticed
in a crowded room. Tell lies:
I love you. I'll be back in half an hour.
I'm fine.

The childish things.
Stand very still behind a tree,
become a cowboy, say you have died,
climb into wardrobes, breathe on a mirror
until there's no one there, and practise magic,
tricks with smoke and fire –

a flick of the wrist and the victim's lost
his watch, his wife, his ten pound note. Perfect it.
Hold your breath a little longer every time.

The hardest things.
Eat less, much less, and take a vow of silence.
Learn the point of vanishing, the moment
embers turn to ash, the sun falls down,
the sudden white-out comes.
And when it comes again – it will –
just walk at it, walk into it, and walk,
until you know that you're no longer
anywhere.

What Are Heavy?

Christina Rossetti
(1830–1894)

What are heavy? Sea-sand and sorrow;
What are brief? Today and tomorrow;
What are frail? Spring blossoms and youth;
What are deep? The ocean and truth.

The Lamplighter

Robert Louis Stevenson
(1850–1894)

A lamplighter is someone who used to light gas lamps in cities and towns before the invention of electricity. In Robert Louis Stevenson's poem, the lamplighter is called Leerie and this became another word for lamplighter in Scotland – that's how famous the poem was. It's thought Stevenson was very ill as a child and had to spend a lot of time on his own, like the child in this poem, watching Leerie go past lighting the lamps, his imagination captured by the man 'with lantern and ladder'.

★★★

My tea is nearly ready and the sun has left the sky;
It's time to take the window to see Leerie going by;
For every night at tea-time and before you take your seat,
With lantern and with ladder he comes posting up the street.

Now Tom would be a driver and Maria go to sea,
And my papa's a banker and as rich as he can be;
But I, when I am stronger and can choose what I'm to do,
O Leerie, I'll go round at night and light the lamps with you!

For we are very lucky, with a lamp before the door,
And Leerie stops to light it as he lights so many more;
And O! before you hurry by with ladder and with light,
O Leerie, see a little child and nod to him to-night!

The Arrow and the Song

H W Longfellow
(1807–1882)

I shot an arrow into the air,
It fell to earth, I knew not where;
For, so swiftly it flew, the sight
Could not follow it in its flight.

I breathed a song into the air,
It fell to earth, I knew not where;
For who has sight so keen and strong,
That it can follow the flight of song?

Long, long afterward, in an oak
I found the arrow, still unbroke;
And the song, from beginning to end,
I found again in the heart of a friend.

My Shadow

Robert Louis Stevenson
(1850–1894)

I have a little shadow that goes in and out with me,
And what can be the use of him is more than I can see.
He is very, very like me from the heels up to the head;
And I see him jump before me, when I jump into my bed.

The funniest thing about him is the way he likes to grow –
Not at all like proper children, which is always very slow;
For he sometimes shoots up taller like an india-rubber ball,
And he sometimes gets so little that there's none of him at all.

He hasn't got a notion of how children ought to play,
And can only make a fool of me in every sort of way.
He stays so close behind me, he's a coward you can see;
I'd think shame to stick to nursie as that shadow sticks to me!

One morning, very early, before the sun was up,
I rose and found the shining dew on every buttercup;
But my lazy little shadow, like an arrant sleepy-head,
Had stayed at home behind me and was fast asleep in bed.

Poem de terre

John Hegley
(1953–)

John Hegley is a poet, singer and songwriter from Luton. Hegley has French relatives if you look back far enough into his family history (his father's name was René) and he often writes about this. This poem draws inspiration from the French word for potato ('pomme de terre' – the 'apple of the earth') but adds a bit of a twist. What words in other languages do you like best?

★★★

I'm not a normal person
whatever that may be
there is something very very vegetable
about me,
this human skin I'm skulking in
it's only there for show,
I'm a potato.
When I told my father
it was something of a blow,
he was hurt
and he called me a dirty so-and-so.
He kicked up a racket
and he grabbed me by the jacket;
I said, 'Daddy will you pack it in
I need you for my father not my foe
Daddy, will you try and help me grow,

won't you love me for my blemishes
and look me in the eye
before one of us is underground
and the other says goodbye?'
And he said 'No'.

When I was a schoolboy
I never knew why
I was so crap at cross-country running
but now I know
why I was so slow.
I'm a potato.

We Real Cool

Gwendolyn Brooks
(1917–2000)

Gwendolyn Brooks was born in Kansas in the USA, and this short, song-like poem is set in 1950s America. At that time, many schools in America were segregated, meaning that children from different ethnic backgrounds had to go to separate schools. The poem explores the reality that many young people would have faced at the time if they decided to leave school. Instead of going to school, the boys at the pool hall are involved in illegal activities – they 'lurk late' (suggesting they hang around after dark), 'strike straight' (they don't get caught for their crimes), 'sing sin' (boast about what they have been up to) and 'thin gin' (water down alcohol and sell it on to make money). Without school, there aren't many options available to them.

★★★

The Pool Players.
Seven at the Golden Shovel.

We real cool. We
Left school. We

Lurk late. We
Strike straight. We

Sing sin. We
Thin gin. We

Jazz June. We
Die soon.

Why Do You Stay Up So Late?

Don Paterson
(1963–)

In this poem, the narrator (a poet) tries to explain to his young son why he stays up late at night writing. Do you think this is a good answer to the question?

***

For Russ

I'll tell you, if you really want to know:
remember that day you lost two years ago
at the rockpool where you sat and played the jeweller
with all those stones you'd stolen from the shore?
Most of them went dark and nothing more,
but sometimes one would blink the secret colour
it had locked up somewhere in its stony sleep.
This is how you knew the ones to keep.

So I collect the dull things of the day
in which I see some possibility
but which are dead and which have the surprise
I don't know, and I've no pool to help me tell –
so I look at them and look at them until
one thing makes a mirror in my eyes

then I paint it with the tear to make it bright.
This is why I sit up through the night.

Invictus

W E Henley
(1849–1903)

Out of the night that covers me,
    Black as the Pit from pole to pole,
I thank whatever gods may be
    For my unconquerable soul.

In the fell clutch of circumstance
    I have not winced nor cried aloud.
Under the bludgeonings of chance
    My head is bloody, but unbowed.

Beyond this place of wrath and tears
    Looms but the Horror of the shade,
And yet the menace of the years
    Finds, and shall find, me unafraid.

It matters not how strait the gate,
    How charged with punishments the scroll,
I am the master of my fate;
    I am the captain of my soul.

'I Am'

John Clare
(1793–1864)

I am – yet what I am, none cares or knows;
　My friends forsake me like a memory lost: –
I am the self-consumer of my woes; –
　They rise and vanish in oblivion's host,
Like shadows in love's frenzied stifled throes: –
And yet I am, and live – like vapours tost

Into the nothingness of scorn and noise, –
　Into the living sea of waking dreams,
Where there is neither sense of life or joys,
　But the vast shipwreck of my lifes esteems;
Even the dearest that I love the best
Are strange – nay, rather stranger than the rest.

I long for scenes, where man hath never trod
　A place where woman never smiled or wept
There to abide with my Creator, God;
　And sleep as I in childhood, sweetly slept,
Untroubling, and untroubled where I lie,
The grass below – above the vaulted sky.

Fashion

Benjamin Zephaniah
(1958–)

It's stylish to have false dreadlocks,
It's stylish to have different sox,
It's stylish to have gloves wid holes
They say it's sexy to have moles.
Fashions change, fashions are strange,
Designers just design a range,
And at de store people want more,
That's what they've earnt their money for.
Few dictate, most imitate
So stylish, till they're out of date,
But what gets me mad more and more
Is, now it's stylish to look poor.

The New Colossus

Emma Lazarus
(1849–1887)

Not like the brazen giant of Greek fame,
With conquering limbs astride from land to land;
Here at our sea-washed, sunset gates shall stand
A mighty woman with a torch, whose flame
Is the imprisoned lightning, and her name
Mother of Exiles. From her beacon-hand
Glows world-wide welcome; her mild eyes command
The air-bridged harbor that twin cities frame.
'Keep, ancient lands, your storied pomp!' cries she
With silent lips. 'Give me your tired, your poor,
Your huddled masses yearning to breathe free,
The wretched refuse of your teeming shore.
Send these, the homeless, tempest-tost to me,
I lift my lamp beside the golden door!'

Thought

D H Lawrence
(1885–1930)

Thought, I love thought.
But not the jaggling and twisting of already existent ideas
I despise that self-important game.
Thought is the welling up of unknown life into consciousness,
Thought is the testing of statements on the touchstone of the
    conscience,
Thought is gazing on to the face of life, and reading what
    can be read,
Thought is pondering over experience, and coming to
    conclusion.
Thought is not a trick, or an exercise, or a set of dodges,
Thought is a man in his wholeness wholly attending.

Items Carried Up Ben Nevis

Helen Mort
(1985–)

The piano, that was easiest, despite the keys
rattling like dice beneath the lid, so next
I strapped a toffee-coloured horse across my back,
ferried a coffin with the body still inside
pitching from left to right with every move.

I took a statue of Napoleon and set it
on the pony track – a kind of shrine –
and goaded later in the pub, I dragged
the whole place up with me, stopped
to pull a pint beneath the summit cairn.

By then, the town was a skeleton,
the mountain curtseying with weight,
which just left you: I draped your arms
around my neck. Light as you are,
I couldn't take you with me. Not a step.

The First Men on Mercury

Edwin Morgan
(1920–2010)

– We come in peace from the third planet.
Would you take us to your leader?

– Bawr stretter! Bawr. Bawr. Stretterhawl?

– This is a little plastic model
of the solar system, with working parts.
You are here and we are there and we
are now here with you, is this clear?

– Gawl horrop. Bawr. Abawrhannahanna!

– Where we come from is blue and white
with brown, you see we call the brown
here 'land', the blue is 'sea', and the white
is 'clouds' over land and sea, we live
on the surface of the brown land,
all round is sea and clouds. We are 'men'.
Men come –

– Glawp men! Gawrbenner menko. Menhawl?

– Men come in peace from the third planet
which we call 'earth'. We are earthmen.
Take us earthmen to your leader.

– Thmen? Thmen? Bawr. Bawrhossop.
Yuleeda tan hanna. Harrabost yuleeda.

– I am the yuleeda. You see my hands,
we carry no benner, we come in peace.
The spaceways are all stretterhawn.

– Glawn peacemen all horrabhanna tantko!
Tan come at'mstrossop. Glawp yuleeda!

– Atoms are peacegawl in our harraban.
Menbat worrabost from tan hannahanna.

– You men we know bawrhossoptant. Bawr.
We know yuleeda. Go strawg backspetter quick.

– We cantantabawr, tantingko backspetter now!

– Banghapper now! Yes, third planet back.
Yuleeda will go back blue, white, brown
nowhanna! There is no more talk.

– Gawl han fasthapper?

– No. You must go back to your planet.
Go back in peace, take what you have gained
but quickly.

– Stretterworra gawl, gawl …

– Of course, but nothing is ever the same,
now is it? You'll remember Mercury.

O Captain! My Captain!

Walt Whitman
(1819–1892)

Walt Whitman was an American poet, writer and journalist, who closely followed the political issues of his time. This poem mourns the death of the American President, Abraham Lincoln, after he was assassinated in a theatre in 1865.

The poem is an 'elegy', which means it is a poem of mourning. It uses the metaphor of a ship (representing the USA) of which Abraham Lincoln is the captain.

★★★

O Captain! my Captain! Our fearful trip is done,
The ship has weather'd every rack, the prize we sought is won;
The port is near, the bells I hear, the people all exulting,
While follow eyes the steady keel, the vessel grim and daring;
　　But O heart! heart! heart!
　　　　O the bleeding drops of red,
　　　　　　Where on the deck my Captain lies,
　　　　　　　　Fallen cold and dead.

O Captain! my Captain! Rise up and hear the bells;
Rise up – for you the flag is flung – for you the bugle trills,
For you bouquets and ribbon'd wreaths – for you the shores
　　a-crowding;

For you they call, the swaying mass, their eager faces turning;
   Here Captain! dear father!
      The arm beneath your head!
         It is some dream that on the deck,
            You've fallen cold and dead.

My Captain does not answer, his lips are pale and still;
My father does not feel my arm, he has no pulse nor will;
The ship is anchor'd safe and sound, its voyage closed and done;
From fearful trip, the victor ship, comes in with object won;
   Exult O shores, and ring O bells!
      But I with mournful tread,
         Walk the deck my Captain lies,
            Fallen cold and dead.

A Smuggler's Song

Rudyard Kipling
(1865–1936)

Rudyard Kipling was born in India and grew up in England. He is
probably best known for writing *The Jungle Book*. This poem is written
in the voice of a smuggler – someone who would have sneaked
things illegally across a border, a kind of stealing. Smugglers would
have been chased by the king's soldiers (mentioned in the poem as
'King George's men, dressed in blue and red') and, in this poem, the
townsfolk turn a blind eye to what they are up to. Smugglers in famous
stories usually try to sink ships, kill sailors and steal loot. Kipling's
smugglers are a bit less scary and dangerous.

★★★

If you wake at midnight, and hear a horse's feet,
Don't go drawing back the blind, or looking in the street.
Them that asks no questions isn't told a lie.
Watch the wall, my darling, while the Gentlemen go by!
    Five and twenty ponies,
    Trotting through the dark –
    Brandy for the Parson,
    'Baccy for the Clerk;
    Laces for a lady, letters for a spy,
And watch the wall, my darling, while the Gentlemen go by!

Running round the woodlump if you chance to find
Little barrels, roped and tarred, all full of brandy-wine,

Don't you shout to come and look, nor use 'em for your play.
Put the brishwood back again - and they'll be gone next day!

If you see the stable-door setting open wide;
If you see a tired horse lying down inside;
If your mother mends a coat cut about and tore;
If the lining's wet and warm – don't you ask no more!

If you meet King George's men, dressed in blue and red,
You be careful what you say, and mindful what is said.
If they call you 'pretty maid', and chuck you 'neath the chin,
Don't you tell where no one is, nor yet where no one's been!

Knocks and footsteps round the house – whistles after dark –
You've no call for running out till the house-dogs bark.
Trusty's here, and *Pincher's* here, and see how dumb they lie –
They don't fret to follow when the Gentlemen go by!

If you do as you've been told, 'likely there's a chance,
You'll be give a dainty doll, all the way from France,
With a cap of Valenciennes, and a velvet hood –
A present from the Gentlemen, along o' being good!
    Five and twenty ponies,
    Trotting through the dark –
    Brandy for the Parson,
    'Baccy for the Clerk;
Them that asks no questions isn't told a lie –
Watch the wall, my darling, while the Gentlemen go by!

A Martian Sends a Postcard Home

Craig Raine
(1944–)

In the 1970s in Britain, there was a style of poetry called 'Martianism' – poets tried to make familiar things seem a bit strange. The term 'Martianism' came from this poem by Craig Raine – in it, he describes ordinary things (cars and telephones, for example) as if they were being seen by someone from outer space. Can you work out what objects are being described in this poem? What would you say if you could send a postcard to a Martian?

★★★

Caxtons are mechanical birds with many wings
and some are treasured for their markings –

they cause the eyes to melt
or the body to shriek without pain.

I have never seen one fly, but
sometimes they perch on the hand.

Mist is when the sky is tired of flight
and rests its soft machine on ground:

then the world is dim and bookish
like engravings under tissue paper.

Rain is when the earth is television.
It has the property of making colours darker.

Model T is a room with the lock inside –
a key is turned to free the world

for movement, so quick there is a film
to watch for anything missed.

But time is tied to the wrist
or kept in a box, ticking with impatience.

In homes, a haunted apparatus sleeps,
that snores when you pick it up.

If the ghost cries, they carry it
to their lips and soothe it to sleep

with sounds. And yet, they wake it up
deliberately, by tickling with a finger.

Only the young are allowed to suffer
openly. Adults go to a punishment room

with water but nothing to eat.
They lock the door and suffer the noises

alone. No one is exempt
and everyone's pain has a different smell.

At night when all the colours die,
they hide in pairs

and read about themselves –
in colour, with their eyelids shut.

Futility

Wilfred Owen
(1893–1918)

Move him into the sun –
Gently its touch awoke him once,
At home, whispering of fields unsown.
Always it awoke him, even in France,
Until this morning and this snow.
If anything might rouse him now
The kind old sun will know.

Think how it wakes the seeds –
Woke, once, the clays of a cold star.
Are limbs so dear-achieved, are sides
Full-nerved, – still warm, – too hard to stir?
Was it for this the clay grew tall?
– O what made fatuous sunbeams toil
To break earth's sleep at all?

Here Dead Lie We

A E Housman
(1859–1936)

Here dead lie we
Because we did not choose
To live and shame the land
From which we sprung.

Life, to be sure,
Is nothing much to lose,
But young men think it is,
And we were young.

Dulce et Decorum est

Wilfred Owen
(1893–1918)

This poem was written during the First World War. The words *Dulce et Decorum est* are Latin and mean 'it is sweet and glorious'. The phrase 'it is sweet and glorious to die for one's country' was often quoted during the war to encourage people to fight.

A gruesome weapon used in the war was chlorine gas. In this poem Owen describes a gas attack in graphic detail. He uses a lot of harsh consonant sounds to convey the brutality of combat. Try reading the poem out loud to hear this effect in action.

Owen himself was killed in 1918, just one week before the end of the war.

★★★

Bent double, like old beggars under sacks,
Knock-kneed, coughing like hags, we cursed through sludge,
Till on the haunting flares we turned our backs,
And towards our distant rest began to trudge.
Men marched asleep. Many had lost their boots,
But limped on, blood-shod. All went lame, all blind;
Drunk with fatigue; deaf even to the hoots
Of gas-shells dropping softly behind.

Gas! GAS! Quick, boys! – An ecstasy of fumbling
Fitting the clumsy helmets just in time,
But someone still was yelling out and stumbling
And flound'ring like a man in fire or lime. –
Dim through the misty panes and thick green light,
As under a green sea, I saw him drowning.

In all my dreams before my helpless sight
He plunges at me, guttering, choking, drowning.

If in some smothering dreams, you too could pace
Behind the wagon that we flung him in,
And watch the white eyes writhing in his face,
His hanging face, like a devil's sick of sin,
If you could hear, at every jolt, the blood
Come gargling from the froth-corrupted lungs
Bitten as the cud
Of vile, incurable sores on innocent tongues, –
My friend, you would not tell with such high zest
To children ardent for some desperate glory,
The old Lie: *Dulce et decorum est*
Pro patria mori.

The Charge of the Light Brigade

Alfred, Lord Tennyson
(1809–1892)

Alfred Tennyson was Poet Laureate to Queen Victoria, meaning he was expected to write poems for big national occasions. He wrote this poem about a charge by British cavalry forces (the Light Brigade) at the Battle of Balaclava in the Crimean War in October 1854. A message wasn't delivered properly and the Light Brigade was sent to charge at a very well-armed artillery battery – many of them died. Tennyson praises the men of the Light Brigade for their bravery, but he is also sad about what happened.

Read some of Tennyson's poem aloud – you'll notice how he repeats things several times. The rhythm and repetition of the lines makes them sound like horses' hooves striking the ground. When you read the poem, you can hear the Light Brigade as well as picture them.

★★★

Half a league, half a league,
   Half a league onward,
All in the valley of Death
   Rode the six hundred.
'Forward, the Light Brigade!
Charge for the guns!' he said:
Into the valley of Death
   Rode the six hundred.

'Forward, the Light Brigade!'
Was there a man dismay'd?
Not tho' the soldier knew
    Some one had blunder'd:
Their's not to make reply,
Their's not to reason why,
Their's but to do and die:
Into the valley of Death
    Rode the six hundred.

Cannon to right of them,
Cannon to left of them,
Cannon in front of them
    Volley'd and thunder'd;
Storm'd at with shot and shell,
Boldly they rode and well,
Into the jaws of Death,
Into the mouth of Hell
    Rode the six hundred.

Flash'd all their sabres bare,
Flash'd as they turn'd in air
Sabring the gunners there,
Charging an army, while
    All the world wonder'd:
Plunged in the battery-smoke
Right thro' the line they broke;
Cossack and Russian
Reel'd from the sabre-stroke
    Shatter'd and sunder'd.

Then they rode back, but not,
    Not the six hundred.

Cannon to right of them,
Cannon to left of them,
Cannon behind them
    Volley'd and thunder'd;
Storm'd at with shot and shell,
While horse and hero fell,
They that had fought so well
Came thro' the jaws of Death,
Back from the mouth of Hell,
All that was left of them,
    Left of six hundred.

When can their glory fade?
O the wild charge they made!
    All the world wonder'd.
Honour the charge they made!
Honour the Light Brigade,
    Noble six hundred!

In Flanders Fields

John McCrae
(1872–1918)

In Flanders fields the poppies blow
Between the crosses, row on row,
    That mark our place; and in the sky
    The larks, still bravely singing, fly
Scarce heard amid the guns below.

We are the Dead. Short days ago
We lived, felt dawn, saw sunset glow,
    Loved and were loved, and now we lie,
        In Flanders fields.

Take up our quarrel with the foe:
To you from failing hands we throw
    The torch; be yours to hold it high.
    If ye break faith with us who die
We shall not sleep, though poppies grow
        In Flanders fields.

Disabled

Wilfred Owen
(1893–1918)

He sat in a wheeled chair, waiting for dark,
And shivered in his ghastly suit of grey,
Legless, sewn short at elbow. Through the park
Voices of boys rang saddening like a hymn,
Voices of play and pleasure after day,
Till gathering sleep had mothered them from him.

About this time Town used to swing so gay
When glow-lamps budded in the light-blue trees
And girls glanced lovelier as the air grew dim,
– In the old times, before he threw away his knees.
Now he will never feel again how slim
Girls' waists are, or how warm their subtle hands,
All of them touch him like some queer disease.

There was an artist silly for his face,
For it was younger than his youth, last year.
Now he is old; his back will never brace;
He's lost his colour very far from here,
Poured it down shell-holes till the veins ran dry,
And half his lifetime lapsed in the hot race,
And leap of purple spurted from his thigh.
One time he liked a bloodsmear down his leg,
After the matches carried shoulder-high.
It was after football, when he'd drunk a peg,

He thought he'd better join. He wonders why ...
Someone had said he'd look a god in kilts.

That's why; and maybe, too, to please his Meg,
Aye, that was it, to please the giddy jilts,
He asked to join. He didn't have to beg;
Smiling they wrote his lie; aged nineteen years.
Germans he scarcely thought of; and no fears
Of Fear came yet. He thought of jewelled hilts
For daggers in plaid socks; of smart salutes;
And care of arms; and leave; and pay arrears;
Esprit de corps; and hints for young recruits.
And soon, he was drafted out with drums and cheers.

Some cheered him home, but not as crowds cheer Goal.
Only a solemn man who brought him fruits
Thanked him; and then inquired about his soul.
Now, he will spend a few sick years in Institutes,
And do what things the rules consider wise,
And take whatever pity they may dole.
To-night he noticed how the women's eyes
Passed from him to the strong men that were whole.
How cold and late it is! Why don't they come
And put him into bed? Why don't they come?

The Soldier

Rupert Brooke
(1887–1915)

Rupert Brooke's 'The Soldier' presents an optimistic picture of war – the soldier in the poem suggests that it is an honour to die for your country, since the sacrifice is for the land and people. It was written at the beginning of the First World War in 1914. Attitudes to war changed a great deal as the conflict progressed. Few realized just how dreadful combat really was. In truth, many soldiers believed the war would be over in a few weeks or months – not years. How does Brooke's poem contrast with Wilfred Owen's 'Dulce et Decorum est'?

Brooke fought in the Royal Naval Volunteer Reserve but died from an infected mosquito bite in 1915, a year after 'The Soldier' was published.

★★★

If I should die, think only this of me:
    That there's some corner of a foreign field
That is for ever England. There shall be
    In that rich earth a richer dust concealed;
A dust whom England bore, shaped, made aware,
    Gave, once, her flowers to love, her ways to roam,
A body of England's, breathing English air,
    Washed by the rivers, blest by suns of home.

And think, this heart, all evil shed away,
   A pulse in the eternal mind, no less
      Gives somewhere back the thoughts by England given;
Her sights and sounds; dreams happy as her day;
   And laughter, learnt of friends; and gentleness,
      In hearts at peace, under an English heaven.

Growing Up

Mirror

Sylvia Plath
(1932–1963)

I am silver and exact. I have no preconceptions.
Whatever I see I swallow immediately
Just as it is, unmisted by love or dislike.
I am not cruel, only truthful –
The eye of a little god, four-cornered.
Most of the time I meditate on the opposite wall.
It is pink, with speckles. I have looked at it so long
I think it is a part of my heart. But it flickers.
Faces and darkness separate us over and over.
Now I am a lake. A woman bends over me,
Searching my reaches for what she really is.
Then she turns to those liars, the candles or the moon.
I see her back, and reflect it faithfully.
She rewards me with tears and an agitation of hands.
I am important to her. She comes and goes.
Each morning it is her face that replaces the darkness.
In me she has drowned a young girl, and in me an old woman
Rises toward her day after day, like a terrible fish.

You Are Old, Father William

Lewis Carroll
(1832–1898)

'You are old, Father William,' the young man said,
'And your hair has become very white;
And yet you incessantly stand on your head –
Do you think, at your age, it is right?'

'In my youth,' Father William replied to his son,
'I feared it might injure the brain;
But, now that I'm perfectly sure I have none,
Why, I do it again and again.'

'You are old,' said the youth, 'as I mentioned before,
And have grown most uncommonly fat;
Yet you turned a back-somersault in at the door –
Pray, what is the reason for that?'

'In my youth,' said the sage, as he shook his grey locks,
'I kept all my limbs very supple
By the use of this ointment – one shilling the box –
Allow me to sell you a couple?'

'You are old,' said the youth, 'and your jaws are too weak
For anything tougher than suet;
Yet you finished the goose, with the bones and the beak –
Pray, how did you manage to do it?'

'In my youth,' said his father, 'I took to the law,
And argued each case with my wife;
And the muscular strength, which it gave to my jaw,
Has lasted the rest of my life.'

'You are old,' said the youth, 'one would hardly suppose
That your eye was as steady as ever;
Yet you balanced an eel on the end of your nose –
What made you so awfully clever?'

'I have answered three questions, and that is enough,'
Said his father; 'don't give yourself airs!
Do you think I can listen all day to such stuff?
Be off, or I'll kick you down stairs!'

If–

Rudyard Kipling
(1865–1936)

'If–' is one of Kipling's most famous poems, and takes the form of
advice to his son. It was written as a tribute to a political leader called
Leander Starr Jameson. Jameson was regarded as a logical and
persuasive man, and Kipling thought that younger people would do
well to model themselves on his character. Who do you consider a
good role model?

★★★

If you can keep your head when all about you
Are losing theirs and blaming it on you,
If you can trust yourself when all men doubt you,
But make allowance for their doubting too;
If you can wait and not be tired by waiting,
Or being lied about, don't deal in lies,
Or being hated, don't give way to hating,
And yet don't look too good, nor talk too wise:

If you can dream – and not make dreams your master;
If you can think – and not make thoughts your aim;
If you can meet with Triumph and Disaster
And treat those two impostors just the same;
If you can bear to hear the truth you've spoken
Twisted by knaves to make a trap for fools,
Or watch the things you gave your life to, broken,

And stoop and build 'em up with worn-out tools:

If you can make one heap of all your winnings
And risk it on one turn of pitch-and-toss,
And lose, and start again at your beginnings
And never breathe a word about your loss;
If you can force your heart and nerve and sinew
To serve your turn long after they are gone,
And so hold on when there is nothing in you
Except the Will which says to them: 'Hold on!'

If you can talk with crowds and keep your virtue,
Or walk with Kings – nor lose the common touch,
If neither foes nor loving friends can hurt you,
If all men count with you, but none too much;
If you can fill the unforgiving minute
With sixty seconds' worth of distance run,
Yours is the Earth and everything that's in it,
And – which is more   you'll be a Man, my son!

I Want to Know

John Drinkwater
(1882–1937)

I want to know why when I'm late
For school, they get into a state,
But if invited out to tea
I mustn't ever early be.

Why, if I'm eating nice and slow,
It's 'Slow-coach, hurry up, you know!'
But if I'm eating nice and quick,
It's 'Gobble-gobble, you'll be sick!'

Why, when I'm walking in the street
My clothes must always be complete,
While at the seaside I can call
It right with nothing on at all.

Why I must always go to bed
When other people don't instead,
And why I have to say good night
Always before I'm ready, quite.

Why seeds grow up instead of down,
Why six pence isn't half a crown,
Why kittens are so quickly cats,
And why the angels have no hats.

It seems, however hard they try,
That nobody can tell me why,
So I know really, I suppose,
As much as anybody knows.

I Remember, I Remember

Thomas Hood
(1799–1845)

In this poem, Thomas Hood contrasts his childhood with the adult world. Hood was particularly fond of playing practical jokes on his family. He once instructed his wife to buy plaice from a fish seller, but warned her not to buy any fish with orange or red spots on it, telling her this was a sign of decomposition. Not knowing that plaice was an orange or red-spotted fish, Mrs Hood refused to buy anything from the fish seller, exclaiming in horror at what she saw!

★★★

I remember, I remember
The house where I was born,
The little window where the sun
Came peeping in at morn;
He never came a wink too soon
Nor brought too long a day;
But now, I often wish the night
Had borne my breath away.

I remember, I remember
The roses, red and white,
The violets, and the lily cups –
Those flowers made of light!
The lilacs where the robin built,
And where my brother set

The laburnum on his birthday, –
The tree is living yet!

I remember, I remember
Where I was used to swing,
And thought the air must rush as fresh
To swallows on the wing;
My spirit flew in feathers then
That is so heavy now,
And summer pools could hardly cool
The fever on my brow.

I remember, I remember
The fir trees dark and high;
I used to think their slender tops
Were close against the sky:
It was a childish ignorance,
But now 'tis little joy
To know I'm farther off from Heaven
Than when I was a boy.

Young and Old

Charles Kingsley
(1819–1875)

Charles Kingsley was born in Devon, the son of a vicar. This poem
is taken from his novel *The Water Babies*, in which a young chimney
sweep called Tom falls into a river and is transformed into a 'water
baby'. Below the surface of the water, he begins a series of adventures
in a world ruled over by fairies. 'Young and Old' looks back on the
joys of youth from the vantage point of old age.

★★★

When all the world is young, lad,
    And all the trees are green;
And every goose a swan, lad,
    And every lass a queen;
Then hey for boot and horse, lad,
    And round the world away:
Young blood must have its course, lad,
    And every dog his day.

When all the world is old, lad,
    And all the trees are brown;
And all the sport is stale, lad,
    And all the wheels run down;

Creep home and take your place there,
    The spent and maimed among:
God grant you find one face there
    You loved when all was young.

Growing

Tony Mitton
(1951–)

Today
you may be small.
But one day
you'll be tall,
like me,
maybe taller.
You won't
fit into your bed.
Your hat
won't fit on your head.
Your feet
will fill up the floor.
You'll have to bend down
to come through the door.
You'll be able to reach
to the highest shelf,
(and I can't do that now,
myself).
Out in the country
the tallest trees
will scratch your ankles
and tickle your knees.
Up in the clouds,
yes, way up there,
the eagles will nest

in your craggy hair.
But they'd better soon find
a safer place
because soon your head
will be up in space.

So I hope you won't be too proud
to bend down
and say hello
to your old home town.
And I hope it won't drive you
utterly mad
to visit your tiny
Mum and Dad.

Old Tongue

Jackie Kay
(1961–)

Jackie Kay was born in Edinburgh to a Scottish mother and a Nigerian father and she was adopted by a Scottish family. She has written poetry, plays and fiction, as well as a book about her search for her natural parents. This poem is about the relationship between the words people use and the places they come from. She shares some of her favourite Scottish words. What words do you use that are special to you and that other people might not understand?

★★★

When I was eight, I was forced south.
Not long after, when I opened
my mouth, a strange thing happened.
I lost my Scottish accent.
Words fell off my tongue:
eedyit, dreich, wabbit, crabbit,
stummer, teuchter, heidbanger,
so you are, so am ur, see you, see ma ma,
shut yer geggie or I'll gie ye the malkie!

My own vowels started to stretch like my bones
and I turned my back on Scotland.
Words disappeared in the dead of the night,
new words marched in: ghastly, awful,
quite dreadful, scones said like stones,

Pokey hats into ice-cream cones.
Oh where did all my words go –
my old words, my lost words?
Did you ever feel sad when you lost a word,
did you ever try to call it back
like calling in the sea?
If I could have found my words wandering,
I swear I would have taken them in,
swallowed them whole, knocked them back.

Out in the English soil, my old words
buried themselves. It made my mother's blood boil.
I cried one day with the wrong sound in my mouth.
I wanted them back; I wanted my old accent back,
my old tongue. My dour, soor Scottish tongue.
Sing-songy. *I wanted to gie it laldie.*

First Fig

Edna St Vincent Millay
(1892–1950)

Edna St Vincent Millay's poem, 'First Fig', is about living life to the full while you're young: a candle might burn out quickly, but it gives a 'lovely light'. She seems to be suggesting that it's better to live dangerously than play it safe. What do you think?

★★★

My candle burns at both ends;
    It will not last the night;
But ah, my foes, and oh, my friends –
    It gives a lovely light.

History
and Legend

Robin Hood

John Keats
(1795–1821)

To A Friend

No! those days are gone away,
And their hours are old and grey,
And their minutes buried all
Under the down-trodden pall
Of the leaves of many years;
Many times have winter's shears,
Frozen North, and chilling East,
Sounded tempests to the feast
Of the forest's whispering fleeces,
Since men knew nor rent nor leases.

No, the bugle sounds no more,
And the twanging bow no more;
Silent is the ivory shrill
Past the heath and up the hill;
There is no mid-forest laugh,
Where lone Echo gives the half
To some wight, amazed to hear
Jesting, deep in forest drear.

On the fairest time of June
You may go, with sun or moon,
Or the seven stars to light you,

Or the polar ray to right you;
But you never may behold
Little John, or Robin bold;
Never one, of all the clan,
Thrumming on an empty can
Some old hunting ditty, while
He doth his green way beguile
To fair hostess Merriment,
Down beside the pasture Trent;
For he left the merry tale
Messenger for spicy ale.

Gone, the merry morris din;
Gone, the song of Gamelyn;
Gone, the tough-belted outlaw
Idling in the 'grenè shawe';
All are gone away and past!
And if Robin should be cast
Sudden from his turfèd grave,
And if Marian should have
Once again her forest days,
She would weep, and he would craze.
He would swear, for all his oaks,
Fallen beneath the dockyard strokes,
Have rotted on the briny seas;
She would weep that her wild bees
Sang not to her – strange! that honey
Can't be got without hard money!

So it is: yet let us sing,
Honour to the old bow-string!
Honour to the bugle-horn!
Honour to the woods unshorn!
Honour to the Lincoln green!
Honour to the archer keen!
Honour to tight little John,
And the horse he rode upon!
Honour to bold Robin Hood,
Sleeping in the underwood!
Honour to Maid Marian,
And to all the Sherwood-clan!
Though their days have hurried by
Let us two a burden try.

Ozymandias

Percy Bysshe Shelley
(1792–1822)

Percy Bysshe Shelley wrote this poem in competition with another poet when they heard that a piece of a statue of a very great Egyptian Pharaoh (known as Ozymandias) had come to Britain to be kept in a museum. Shelley's poem became very well known, but his rival's was not as successful. In this poem, Shelley says that empires might fall, but art lasts much longer. That was certainly true for him – his poems are still printed and popular today. What things would you put in a time capsule if you could?

★★★

I met a traveller from an antique land
Who said: Two vast and trunkless legs of stone
Stand in the desert. Near them, on the sand,
Half sunk, a shattered visage lies, whose frown,
And wrinkled lip, and sneer of cold command,
Tell that its sculptor well those passions read
Which yet survive, stamped on these lifeless things,
The hand that mocked them and the heart that fed.
And on the pedestal these words appear:
'My name is Ozymandias, king of kings:
Look on my works, ye Mighty, and despair!'
Nothing beside remains. Round the decay
Of that colossal wreck, boundless and bare
The lone and level sands stretch far away.

The Pied Piper of Hamelin
(an extract)

Robert Browning
(1812–1889)

Robert Browning's poem draws on a German tale about children vanishing from a village called Hamelin in the Middle Ages. A man is employed as a rat catcher to get rid of the village's troublesome rats by luring them away with his magic pipe. His music is so beautiful that all the rats follow him out of town. But afterwards, the townsfolk don't pay him. He strikes back, leading their children away with his magical music, just like he did with the rodents.

Look at the steady rhythm of the poem and the rhymes at the end of each line – does it remind you of people marching? The beats of the poem's lines are a bit like the Pied Piper's stamping feet as he plays his tune and leads the children away.

★★★

You should have heard the Hamelin people
Ringing the bells till they rocked the steeple.
'Go,' cried the Mayor, 'and get long poles!
Poke out the nests and block up the holes!
Consult with carpenters and builders,
And leave in our town not even a trace
Of the rats!' – when suddenly up the face
Of the Piper perked in the market-place,

With a, 'First, if you please, my thousand guilders!'

A thousand guilders! The Mayor looked blue;
So did the Corporation, too.
For council dinners made rare havoc
With Claret, Moselle, Vin-de-Grave, Hock;
And half the money would replenish
Their cellar's biggest butt with Rhenish.
To pay this sum to a wandering fellow
With a gypsy coat of red and yellow!
'Beside,' quoth the Mayor, with a knowing wink,
'Our business was done at the river's brink;
We saw with our eyes the vermin sink,
And what's dead can't come to life, I think.
So, friend, we're not the folks to shrink
From the duty of giving you something for drink,
And a matter of money to put in your poke;
But as for the guilders, what we spoke
Of them, as you very well know, was in joke.
Beside, our losses have made us thrifty;
A thousand guilders! Come, take fifty!'

The Piper's face fell, and he cried,
'No trifling! I can't wait! Beside,
I've promised to visit by dinner-time
Bagdat, and accept the prime
Of the Head Cook's pottage, all he's rich in,
For having left, in the Caliph's kitchen,
Of a nest of scorpions no survivor, –
With him I proved no bargain-driver,

With you, don't think I'll bate a stiver!
And folks who put me in a passion
May find me pipe to another fashion.'

'How?' cried the Mayor, 'd'ye think I'll brook
Being worse treated than a Cook?
Insulted by a lazy ribald
With idle pipe and vesture piebald?
You threaten us, fellow? Do your worst,
Blow your pipe there till you burst!'

Once more he stept into the street,
    And to his lips again
    Laid his long pipe of smooth straight cane;
And ere he blew three notes (such sweet
Soft notes as yet musician's cunning
    Never gave the enraptured air)
There was a rustling, that seemed like a bustling
Of merry crowds justling at pitching and hustling;
Small feet were pattering, wooden shoes clattering,
Little hands clapping and little tongues chattering;
And, like fowls in a farm-yard when barley is scattering,
Out came the children running:
All the little boys and girls,
With rosy cheeks and flaxen curls,
And sparkling eyes and teeth like pearls,
Tripping and skipping, ran merrily after
The wonderful music with shouting and laughter.

The Mayor was dumb, and the Council stood
As if they were changed into blocks of wood,
Unable to move a step, or cry
To the children merrily skipping by, –
And could only follow with the eye
That joyous crowd at the Piper's back.
But how the Mayor was on the rack,
And the wretched Council's bosoms beat,
As the Piper turned from the High Street
To where the Weser rolled its waters
Right in the way of their sons and daughters!

Jerusalem

William Blake
(1757–1827)

This poem by Blake is now best known as a song – it was set to music by Sir Hubert Parry in 1916. It was inspired by a story that suggested Jesus once travelled to England and visited the south-west of the country. In his poem, Blake imagines Jesus creating a new heaven in England. Do you know any other poems that have become songs? Or are there songs that you think are a bit like poems? Why not try singing a poem in this book to your favourite tune?

***

And did those feet in ancient time
Walk upon England's mountains green?
And was the holy Lamb of God
On England's pleasant pastures seen?

And did the countenance divine
Shine forth upon our clouded hills?
And was Jerusalem builded here
Among these dark satanic mills?

Bring me my bow of burning gold!
Bring me my arrows of desire!
Bring me my spear! O clouds, unfold!
Bring me my chariot of fire!

I will not cease from mental fight,
Nor shall my sword sleep in my hand,
Till we have built Jerusalem
In England's green and pleasant land.

The Song of Wandering Aengus

William Butler Yeats
(1865–1939)

In Irish mythology, Aengus was supposed to be the god of love, youth and poetic inspiration. In the poem, Aengus is found wandering, looking for his lover, a girl who he had seen in his dreams. This poem reflects Yeats' interest in Celtic folktales.

***

I went out to the hazel wood,
Because a fire was in my head,
And cut and peeled a hazel wand,
And hooked a berry to a thread;
And when white moths were on the wing,
And moth-like stars were flickering out,
I dropped the berry in a stream
And caught a little silver trout.

When I had laid it on the floor
I went to blow the fire a-flame,
But something rustled on the floor,
And someone called me by my name:
It had become a glimmering girl
With apple blossom in her hair
Who called me by my name and ran
And faded through the brightening air.

Though I am old with wandering
Through hollow lands and hilly lands,
I will find out where she has gone,
And kiss her lips and take her hands;
And walk among long dappled grass,
And pluck till time and times are done,
The silver apples of the moon,
The golden apples of the sun.

Ode

Arthur O'Shaughnessy
(1844–1881)

We are the music-makers,
And we are the dreamers of dreams,
Wandering by lone sea-breakers,
And sitting by desolate streams;
World-losers and world-forsakers,
Upon whom the pale moon gleams:
Yet we are the movers and shakers
Of the world for ever, it seems.

With wonderful deathless ditties
We build up the world's great cities,
And out of a fabulous story
We fashion an empire's glory:
One man with a dream, at pleasure,
Shall go forth and conquer a crown;
And three with a new song's measure
Can trample an empire down.

We, in the ages lying
In the buried past of the earth,
Built Nineveh with our sighing,
And Babel itself with our mirth;

And o'erthrew them with prophesying
To the old of the new world's worth;
For each age is a dream that is dying,
Or one that is coming to birth.

Acknowledgements

The author and publishers are grateful to the following for permission to use material that is in copyright:

Bishop, Elizabeth: 'The Fish' from *The Complete Poems 1927-1979* by Elizabeth Bishop. Copyright © Alice Helen Methfessel 1979, 1983. Reprinted by permission of Farrar, Straus and Giroux, LLC.

Brooks, Gwendolyn: 'We Real Cool'. Reprinted by consent of Brooks Permissions.

Cope, Wendy: 'The Uncertainty of the Poet' from *Two Cures For Love* (Faber and Faber, 2009). Reprinted by permission of United Agents on behalf of Wendy Cope.

Copus, Julia: 'The Back Seat Of My Mother's Car' from *The Shuttered Eye* (Bloodaxe Books, 1995).

Dalton, Amanda: 'How To Disappear' from *How to Disappear* (Bloodaxe Books, 1999).

Duffy, Carol Ann: 'Valentine' Copyright © Carol Ann Duffy 1993. Reproduced by permission of the author c/o Rogers, Coleridge & White Ltd., 20 Powis Mews, London W11 1JN.

Heaney, Seamus: 'Death Of A Naturalist' from *Opened Ground*. Reproduced by permission of Faber and Faber Ltd.

Hegley, John: 'Poem de Terre' from *Beyond Our Kennel* (Methuen, 1999).

Kay, Jackie: 'Old Tongue' from *Darling: New & Selected Poems* (Bloodaxe Books, 2007).

Kingsley, Charles: 'Young and Old' by permission of Dr P A K Covey-Crump.

McMillan, Ian: 'Cautionary Playground Rhyme' © Ian McMillan.

Mitton, Tony: 'Growing' from *Plum* (1998).

Morgan, Edwin: 'The Computer's
First Christmas Card' and 'The
First Men On Mercury' from
Collected Poems (Carcanet, 1996).
Reproduced by permission of
Carcanet Press Limited.

Mort, Helen: 'Items Carried
Up Ben Nevis' from *Division
Street*. Published by Chatto
and Windus. Reprinted by
permission of The Random
House Group Limited.

Paterson, Don: 'Why Do You
Stay Up So Late?' Copyright ©
Don Paterson 2009. Reproduced
by permission of the author c/o
Rogers, Coleridge & White Ltd.,
20 Powis Mews, London W11
1JN.

Plath, Sylvia: 'Mirror' from
Collected Poems. Reproduced
by permission of Faber and
Faber Ltd.

Pollard, Clare: 'Tam Lin's Wife'
from *Changeling* (Bloodaxe
Books, 2011).

Raine, Craig: 'A Martian Sends
a Postcard Home'. Copyright ©
Craig Raine, 1979.

Zephaniah, Benjamin: 'Fashion'
(Copyright © Benjamin
Zephaniah) is reproduced by
permission of United Agents
(www.unitedagents.co.uk) on
behalf of Benjamin Zephaniah.

Glossary of Poetic Terms

Here are a few definitions to help you get as much enjoyment as possible out of the poems in this book, so that you can look at the poems in a bit more detail. Can you can find any of these in action?

ALLITERATION – Alliteration is the repetition of the same sound, usually at the beginning of words such as: 'Pied Piper' or 'lizards like leaping'. What effect this has depends on what letter or sound is being repeated.

FORM – The form of a poem is its structure; how it has been built out of words and how it appears on the page. When people talk about form they might be talking about how many verses a poem has, how many lines there are in each verse, whether it rhymes and what its rhythm is like.

METER – When we speak we use a combination of stressed and unstressed syllables. For example, 'cat' is just a single, stressed syllable, but 'sighing' is a stressed syllable followed by an unstressed one. It's all about where the emphasis of the word falls when you say it aloud. Poets can arrange these stresses and non-stresses into patterns to create different rhythms in their poetry, and this is called the meter of the poem.

ONOMATOPOEIA – If a word is onomatopoeic it means that it actually sounds like the thing it is describing. This section from 'The Pied Piper of Hamelin' by Robert Browning is full of onomatopoeia:

There was a rustling that seemed like a bustling
Of merry crowds justling at pitching and hustling,
Small feet were pattering, wooden shoes clattering,
Little hands clapping, and little tongues chattering …

Which words do you think are onomatopoeic? Think about the sounds clothes make when you move, or the sound you hear when you walk.

PERSONIFICATION – Personification is giving human emotions or actions to an animal or thing.

RHYME – Rhyme is when two different words are made up of corresponding sounds that make the words sound alike when you hear them out loud, such as 'tree' and 'sea', or 'letter' and 'better'. Rhyme is used all the time in poetry (often at the end of lines) for many reasons. It can be used to generate pace, alter the rhythm, to create humour and to emphasize something. But remember, not all poems have to rhyme.

Often when people talk about rhyme in poetry they talk about rhyme schemes. This is how a poet organizes rhyme in their poems. Look at this verse from 'The Donkey' by G K Chesterton:

When fishes flew and forests walked	a
And figs grew upon thorn,	b
Some moment when the moon was blood	c
Then surely I was born.	b

Here pairs of words that rhyme are given the same letter, so we would say the rhyme scheme of this verse is abcb. Looking at rhyme this way makes it easier to notice patterns and consider their effect.

RHYTHM – The rhythm of a poem is its beat, which is created by the poet using a pattern of stressed or unstressed syllables. A stressed syllable is one which is emphasized in a word, and an unstressed syllable is one that is not.

SIMILE   A simile is a direct comparison between two things that often uses either 'like' or 'as' to make the comparison, such as when William Wordsworth says: *I wandered lonely as a cloud*, or in 'Mirror' when Sylvia Plath describes a reflection appearing *like a terrible fish*.

METAPHOR – A metaphor (like a simile) is an imaginative comparison between two things. However, instead of suggesting one thing is 'like' another, a metaphor insists one thing actually 'is' another. A metaphor can be used for a single image, such as in Carol Ann Duffy's poem 'Valentine': *I give you an onion. / It is a moon wrapped in brown paper* ... or for an entire poem, such as in Edna St Vincent Millay's 'First Fig'. The poem seems to be about a candle, but really the candle is a metaphor for life.

SONNET – A sonnet is a poem that consists of 14 lines. Shakespearean sonnets are the most famous type of sonnets – they consist of three verses with four lines each and end with two lines that rhyme (known as a 'couplet'). There are lots of other sonnet variations that other poets have used across history.

Index of Authors

Allingham, William   61

Anonymous   32

Bishop, Elizabeth   24

Blake, William   18, 172

Brooke, Rupert   144

Brooks, Gwendolyn   112

Browning, Robert   168

Carroll, Lewis   16, 36, 56, 88, 148

Chesterton, G K   22

Clare, John   10, 50, 117

Cope, Wendy   78

Copus, Julia   96

Dalton, Amanda   104

Donne, John   98

Drinkwater, John   152

Duffy, Carol Ann   92

Hardy, Thomas   40

Heaney, Seamus   30

Hegley, John   110

Henley, W E   116

Hood, Thomas   39, 154

Housman, A E   135

Howitt, Mary   27

Kay, Jackie   160

Keats, John   46, 164

Kingsley, Charles   156

Kipling, Rudyard   128, 150

Lawrence, D H   11, 120

Lazarus, Emma   119

Lear, Edward   8, 20, 71, 74, 80, 86

Longfellow, H W   108

Lowell, Amy   52

McCrae, John   141

McMillan, Ian   72

Millay, Edna St Vincent   45, 162

Mitton, Tony   158

Morgan, Edwin   84, 123

Mort, Helen   4, 122

O'Shaughnessy, Arthur   176

Owen, Wilfred   134, 136, 142

Paterson, Don   4, 114

Plath, Sylvia   147

Pollard, Clare   100

Raine, Craig   130

Rilke, Rainer Maria   34

Rossetti, Christina   35, 44, 64, 106

Shakespeare, William   48, 58, 59, 68, 95

Shelley, Percy Bysshe   167

Stevenson, Robert Louis   49, 107, 109

Tennyson, Alfred, Lord   55, 138

Thomas, Edward   38

Whitman, Walt   126

Wilde, Oscar   60

Wordsworth, William   42, 94

Yeats, William Butler   102, 174

Zephaniah, Benjamin   118

Index of Titles

Afternoon on a Hill	45
Akond of Swat, The	80
Ants, The	10
Arrow and the Song, The	108
As You Like It (an extract from)	48
Back Seat of My Mother's Car, The	96
Bed in Summer	49
Cautionary Playground Rhyme	72
Charge of the Light Brigade, The	138
Composed Upon Westminster Bridge, September 3, 1802	94
Computer's First Christmas Card, The	84
Crocodile, The	36
Death of a Naturalist	30
Disabled	142
Dong with a Luminous Nose, The	74
Donkey, The	22
Duck and the Kangaroo, The	20
Dulce et Decorum est	136
Fairies, The	61
Fashion	118
First Fig	162
First Men on Mercury, The	123
Fish, The	24
Futility	134
Goblin Market (an extract from)	64
Growing	158
Here Dead Lie We	135
How to Disappear	104
Hurt No Living Thing	35
'I Am'	117
I Remember, I Remember	154
I Wandered Lonely as a Cloud	42
I Want to Know	152
If–	150
In Flanders Fields	141
In the Forest	60
Invictus	116
Items Carried Up Ben Nevis	122
Jabberwocky	56
Jerusalem	172
Kraken, The	55
Lamplighter, The	107
Macbeth (an extract from)	68
Mad Gardener's Song, The	88
Martian Sends a Postcard Home, A	130
May	44

Midsummer Night's Dream, A (an extract from)	59
Mirror	147
Mock Turtle's Song, The	16
My Shadow	109
New Colossus, The	119
No!	39
O Captain! My Captain!	126
Ode	176
Old Tongue	160
Owl and the Pussycat, The	8
Ozymandias	167
Panther, The	34
Pied Piper of Hamelin, The (an extract from)	168
Pleasant Sounds	50
Pleiades, The	52
Pobble Who Has No Toes, The	86
Poem de terre	110
Poor Old Lady	32
Robin Hood	164
Smuggler's Song, A	128
Snake	11
Soldier, The	144
Song of Wandering Aengus, The	174
Sonnet 73	95
Spider and the Fly, The	27
Sun Rising, The	98

Tall Nettles	38
Tam Lin's Wife	100
Tempest, The (an extract from)	58
There Was an Old Man with a Beard	71
Thought	120
To Autumn	46
Tyger, The	18
Uncertainty of the Poet, The	78
Valentine	92
We Real Cool	112
Weathers	40
What Are Heavy?	106
When You Are Old	102
Why Do You Stay Up So Late?	114
You Are Old, Father William	148
Young and Old	156

Index of First Lines

A snake came to my water-trough — 11

All year the flax-dam festered in the heart — 30

And did those feet in ancient time — 172

Be not afeard; the isle is full of noises — 58

Below the thunders of the upper deep — 55

Bent double, like old beggars under sacks — 136

Busy old fool, unruly Sun — 98

By day you cannot see the sky — 52

Caxtons are mechanical birds with many wings — 130

Earth has not anything to show more fair — 94

First rehearse the easy things. — 104

Half a league, half a league — 138

He sat in a wheeled chair, waiting for dark — 142

He thought he saw an Elephant — 88

Here dead lie we — 135

His vision, from the constantly passing bars — 34

How doth the little crocodile — 36

Hurt no living thing — 35

I am a poet. — 78

I am silver and exact. I have no preconceptions. — 147

I am – yet what I am, none cares or knows — 117

I cannot tell you how it was — 44

I caught a tremendous fish — 24

I have a little shadow that goes in and out with me — 109

I met a traveller from an antique land — 167

I remember, I remember — 154

I shot an arrow into the air — 108

I wandered lonely as a cloud — 42

I want to know why when I'm late — 152

I went out to the hazel wood — 174

I will be the gladdest thing — 45

If I should die, think only this of me — 144

If we shadows have offended — 59

If you can keep your head when all about you — 150

If you wake at midnight, and hear a horse's feet — 128

I'll tell you, if you really want to know — 114

I'm not a normal person — 110

In Flanders fields the poppies blow — 141

In winter I get up at night — 49

It's stylish to have false dreadlocks — 118

jollymerry — 84

Morning and evening — 64

Move him into the sun — 134

My candle burns at both ends — 162

The Owl and the Pussycat

My tea is nearly ready and the sun has left the sky	107
Natasha Green	72
No sun – no moon!	39
No! those days are gone away	164
Not a red rose or a satin heart.	92
Not like the brazen giant of Greek fame	119
O Captain! my Captain! Our fearful trip is done	126
Out of the mid-wood's twilight	60
Out of the night that covers me	116
Poor old lady, she swallowed a fly.	32
Round about the cauldron go	68
Said the Duck to the Kangaroo	20
Season of mists and mellow fruitfulness	46
Tall nettles cover up, as they have done	38
That time of year thou mayst in me behold	95
The Owl and the Pussycat went to sea	8
The piano, that was easiest, despite the keys	122
The Pobble who has no toes	86
The Pool Players.	112
The rustling of leaves under the feet in woods and under hedges	50
There was an Old Man with a beard	71
They sat us in a pale and private place	100
This is the weather the cuckoo likes	40
Thought, I love thought.	120
Today	158
'Twas brillig, and the slithy toves	56
Tyger Tyger, burning bright	18
Under the greenwood tree	48
Up the airy mountain	61
We are the music-makers	176
– We come in peace from the third planet.	123
We left before I had time	96
What are heavy? Sea-sand and sorrow	106
What wonder strikes the curious, while he views	10
When all the world is young, lad	156
When awful darkness and silence reign	74
When fishes flew and forests walked	22
When I was eight, I was forced south.	160
When you are old and grey and full of sleep	102
WHO, or why, or which, or what	80
'Will you walk a little faster?' said a whiting to a snail	16
'Will you walk into my parlour?' said the Spider to the Fly	27
'You are old, Father William,' the young man said	148
You should have heard the Hamelin people	168

Index of Well-Known Lines

accent: I lost my Scottish a. 160

age: For each a. is a dream that is dying 177

albatross: He thought he saw an A. 89

ambition: Who doth a. shun 48

ant: The black a.'s city, by a rotten tree 10

apples: A. and quinces 64

The silver a. of the moon 175

arrow: I shot an a. into the air 108

arrows: Bring me my a. of desire! 172

ash: embers turn to a., the sun falls down 105

asleep: Men marched a. 136

bananas: I am a poet of b. 78

bars: a thousand b.; and behind the b., no world 34

beard: a five-haired b. of wisdom 26

There was an Old Man with a b. 71

bed: I have to go to b. by day. 49

the thornies set / In his b. at night. 62

This b. thy center is, these walls, thy sphere. 99

bees: No shade, no shine, no butterflies, no b. 39

beggars: Bent double, like old b. under sacks 136

bell: He tinkledy-blinkledy-winkled a b. 86

bells: Exult O shores, and ring O b.! 127

bird: She swallowed the b. to catch the spider 32

birds: Caxtons are mechanical b. with many wings 130

boat: In a beautiful pea-green b. 8

book: And nodding by the fire, take down this b. 102

borogoves: All mimsy were the b. 56

bow: Bring me my b. of burning gold! 172

bugle: No, the b. sounds no more 164

butterflies: No shade, no shine, no b., no bees 39

candle: My c. burns at both ends 162

cannon: C. to right of them 139

captain: O C.! my C.! Rise up and hear the bells 126

card: Not a cute c. or a kissogram. 93

cat: 'Runcible C. with crimson whiskers!' 87

cauldron: Fire burn, and c. bubble. 68

charge: O the wild c. they made! 140

chariot: Bring me my c. of fire! 172

child: O Leerie, see a little c., and nod to him to-night! 107

children: Out came the c. running 170

circles: As he paces in cramped c. 34

city: This C. now doth, like a garment, wear 94

cliffs: I will look at c. and clouds 45

climb: And c. again the broken bank of my wall-face. 13

cloud: I wandered lonely as a c. 42

cool: We real c. 112

cowboy: become a c., say you have died 104

crocodile: How doth the little c. 36

cruel: I am not c., only truthful 147

cuckoo: This is the weather the c. likes 40

Daddy: I said, 'D. will you pack it in' 110

I was calling to you – D.! – as we screeched away 96

daffodils: A host, of golden d. 42

dance: 'Will you, won't you, will you, won't you, will you join the d.?' 16

dark: He sat in a wheeled chair, waiting for d. 142

day: By d. you cannot see the sky 52

days: No! those d. are gone away 164

dead: Here d. lie we 135
We are the D. 141
You've fallen cold and d. 127

death: D.'s second self, that seals up all in rest. 95
Into the valley of D. 138

devil: The d.'s walking parody 22

dew: when the / d. flashes from its brown feathers! 51

die: If I should d., think only this of me 144

disaster: If you can meet with Triumph and D. 150

dog: And every d. his day. 156

Dong: 'The D. with a luminous Nose!' 75

dragon: Scale of d., tooth of wolf 69

dreadlocks: It's stylish to have false d. 118

dream: For each age is a d. that is dying 177
If you can d. – and not make dreams your master 150
No more yielding but a d. 59

dreams: And we are the dreamers of d. 176

duck: Said the D. to the Kangaroo 20

east: Frozen North, and chilling E. 164

eel: Yet you balanced an e. on the end of your nose 149

elephant: He thought he saw an E. 88

elm: Only the e. butt tops the nettles now. 38

England: A body of E.'s, breathing English air 144
Walk upon E.'s mountains green? 172

eye: What immortal hand or e. 18

eyes: And watch the white e. writhing in his face 137
Burnt the fire of thine e.? 18

face: His hanging f., like a devil's sick of sin 137

fate: I am the master of my f. 116

faun: Flashes my F.! 60

fear: and no fears / Of F. came yet. 143
For f. of little men 61

feathers: when the / dew flashes from its brown f.! 51

feet: And did those f. in ancient time 172
And palms before my f. 23
and what dread f.? 18

fez: Does he wear a turban, a f. or a hat? 80

field: That there's some corner of a foreign f. 144

fields: In Flanders f. 141

fire: Bring me my chariot of f! 172
Burnt the f. of thine eyes? 18
F. burn, and cauldron bubble. 68

fish: And I let the f. go. 26
I caught a tremendous f. 24
Rises toward her day after day, like a terrible f. 147

fishes: And welcomes little f. in 36
When f. flew and forests walked 22

flax: F. had rotted there 30

flowers: I will touch a hundred f. 45

fly: Poor old lady, she swallowed a f. 32
'Will you walk into my parlour?' said the Spider to the F. 27

folk: Wee f., good f. 61

forest: Of the f.'s whispering fleeces 165

forests: In the f. of the night 18
When fishes flew and f. walked 22

frame: Dare f. thy fearful symmetry? 19

frog: Eye of newt, and toe of f. 68
The daddy f. was called a bullfrog 30

frogs: Right down the dam gross-bellied f. were cocked 31

frogspawn: Of f. that grew like clotted water 30

frozen: F. North, and chilling East 164

garotte: G.? / O the Akond of Swat! 81

gas: G.! G.! Quick, boys! 137

geggie: shut yer g. or I'll gie ye the malkie! 160

gentlemen: Watch the wall, my darling, while the G. go by! 128

ghost: cleanest g. I've ever seen! 73

glen: 'Down the g. tramp little men.' 66
Down the rushy g. 61

goblin: 'We must not look at g. men' 66

goblins: Maids heard the g. cry 64

gourd: To swell the g., and plump the hazel shells 46

greenwood: Under the g. tree 48

grief: a wobbling photo of g. 92

grin: How cheerfully he seems to g. 36

hair: Thy h. soft-lifted by the winnowing wind 46

hand: What dread h.? 18
What immortal h. or eye 18

hat: Does he wear a turban, a fez or a h.? 80

head: If you can keep your h. 150
My h. is bloody, but unbowed. 116

heart: And all that mighty h. is lying still! 94
plunges into the h. and is gone. 34

Heaven: To know I'm farther off from H. 155

Hell: Into the mouth of H. 139

hemlock: Root of h., digged i'th' dark 69

hippopotamus: and found it was / A H. 88

horse: Poor old lady, she swallowed a h. 33

house: The h. where I was born 154

hurt: H. no living thing 35

I: I am – yet what I am, none cares or knows 117

impostors: And treat those two i. just the same 150

instruments: Sometimes a thousand twangling i. 58

isle: Be not afeard; the i. is full of noises 58

Jabberwock: 'Beware the J., my son!' 56

jaws: With gently smiling j.! 36

joy: He chortled in his j. 57

Jubjub bird: 'Beware the J. b., and shun' 56

Jumblies: For the J. came in a Sieve, they did 75

kangaroo: He thought he saw a K. 89
Said the Duck to the K. 20

kings: 'My name is Ozymandias, king of k.' 167
Or walk with K. – nor lose the common touch 151

kraken: The K. sleepeth: faintest sunlights flee 55

lady: Laces for a l., letters for a spy 128

lake: Now I am a l. A woman bends over me 147

lamb: Did he who made the L. make thee? 19

lamp: 'I lift my l. beside the golden door!' 119

lamps: O Leerie, I'll go round at night and light the l. with you! 107

land: In England's green and pleasant l. 173

language: Surely they speak a l. whisperingly 10

lark: The flirt of the ground l.'s wing from the stubbles 51

leader: Take us earthmen to your l. 123

leaves: The rustling of l. under the feet 50

lesson: And take a l. from this tale 29

letters: Laces for a lady, l. for a spy 128

lie: The old L.: *Dulce et decorum est* 137

life: L., to be sure, / Is nothing much to lose 135
'The bitterness of L.!' 88

Light Brigade: 'Forward, the L. B.!' 138

little men: 'Down the glen tramp l. m.' 66
For fear of l. m 61

lonely: I wandered l. as a cloud 42

love: and l. has no conditions. None. 101
To l. that well, which thou must leave ere long. 95

man: And – which is more – you'll be a M., my son! 151

masses: 'Your huddled m. yearning to breathe free' 119

May: When M. was young; ah pleasant M.! 44

Mercury: You'll remember M. 125

mind: A pulse in the eternal m., no less 145

mists: Season of m. and mellow fruitfulness 46

moon: It is a m. wrapped in brown paper. 92
No sun – no m.! 39
Some moment when the m. was blood 22
The silver apples of the m. 175
They danced by the light of the m. 9

morning: The beauty of the m. 94

mountain: the m. curtseying with weight 122
Up the airy m. 61

movers: Yet we are the m. and shakers 176

music: The wonderful m. with shouting and laughter. 170
We are the m.-makers 176

nettles: Tall n. cover up 38

newt: Eye of n., and toe of frog 68

night: This is why I sit up through the n. 115

nightingale: And the little brown n. bills his best 40
O N., catch me his strain! 60

Nile: And pour the waters of the N. 36

north: Frozen N., and chilling East 164

Northern Lights: Of the gay N. L. 62

nose: A N. as strange as a N. could be! 76
Yet you balanced an eel on the end of your n. 149

November: No fruits, no flowers, no leaves, no birds – / N.! 39

ocean: What are deep? The o. and truth. 106

old: And left me o., and cold, and grey. 44

When you are o. and grey 102

'You are o., Father William' 148

onion: I give you an o. 92

owl: The O. and the Pussycat went to sea 8

oysters: Where the Oblong O. grow 75

pain: and everyone's p. has a different smell. 131

palms: And p. before my feet. 23

pancakes: They live on crispy p. 61

parlour: 'Will you walk into my p.?' said the Spider to the Fly 27

parson: Brandy for the P. 128

peaches: Bloom-down-cheeked p. 65

people: No recognitions of familiar p. 39

person: I'm not a normal p. 110

photo: a wobbling p. of grief. 92

piano: The p., that was easiest 122

pipe: 'Blow your p. there till you burst!' 170

Playing a p. with silvery squeaks 76

piper: That joyous crowd at the P.'s back. 171

pit: Black as the P. from pole to pole 116

planet: – Men come in peace from the third p. 123

Pleiades: Papa says they're the P. 52

poet: I am a p. of bananas. 78

pomp: 'Keep, ancient lands, your storied p.!' 119

poor: now it's stylish to look p. 118

poppies: Drowsed with the fume of p. 47

In Flanders fields the p. blow 141

porpoise: 'There's a p. close behind us, and he's treading on my tail.' 16

potato: I'm a p. 110

pulse: A p. in the eternal mind, no less 145

pussycat: The Owl and the P. went to sea 8

remnants: Deformed r. of the Fairy-days. 10

ring: With a r. at the end of his nose 9

Robin: And R. shall restore amends. 59

Robin Hood: Honour to bold R. H. 166

rooks: and r. in families homeward go 41

sands: The lone and level s. stretch far away. 167

season: S. of mists and mellow fruitfulness 46

shade: No s., no shine, no butterflies, no bees 39

shadow: I have a little s. 109

shadows: If we s. have offended 59

Shalott: Like the lady who lived in that isle remote, / S. 82

shine: No shade, no s., no butterflies, no bees 39

shower: Except to prove the sweetness of a s. 38

sieve: 'And they went to sea in a S.' 75

silver: I am s. and exact. I have no preconceptions. 147

sky: By day you cannot see the s. 52

sleep: His ancient, dreamless, uninvaded s. 55

small: Today / you may be s. 158

snail: 'Will you walk a little faster?' said a whiting to a s. 16

snake: A s. came to my water-trough 11

snakes: For in Sicily the black, black s. are innocent, the gold are venomous. 12

soap: A Bar of Mottled S. 90

song: I breathed a s. into the air 108

sores: Of vile, incurable s. on innocent tongues 137

sorrow: What are heavy? Sea-sand and s. 106

soul: I am the captain of my s. 116

south: When I was eight, I was forced s. 160

spark: There moves what seems a fiery s. 74

spider: Poor old lady, she swallowed a s. 32
'Will you walk into my parlour?' said the S. to the Fly 27

spoon: Which they ate with a runcible s. 9

spring: Where are the songs of S.? 47

spy: Laces for a lady, letters for a s. 128

stars: To feel that they had s. for toys! 53

sun: And now the s. has sunk, dark taken hold 101
Busy old Fool, unruly S. 98
embers turn to ash, the s. falls down 105
Move him into the s. 134
My tea is nearly ready and the s. has left the sky 107
Never did s. more beautifully steep 94
No s. – no moon! 39
The golden apples of the s. 175
The kind old s. will know. 134
where the s. / Came peeping in at morn 154

sunset: furious as a s. 97

swallows: And gathering s. twitter in the skies. 47

symmetry: Dare frame thy fearful s.? 19

thought: T., I love t. 120

toes: The Pobble who has no t. 86

toil: Double, double, t. and trouble 68

traveller: I met a t. from an antique land 167

tree: He gathered the bark of the Twangum T. 76

triumph: If you can meet with T. and Disaster 150

trouble: Double, double, toil and t. 68

truth: What are deep? The ocean and t. 106

Tumtum tree: So rested he by the T. t. 56

turban: Does he wear a t., a fez or a hat? 80

twilight: Out of the mid-wood's t. 60

Tyger: T. T., burning bright 18

valley: Into the v. of Death 138

voices: V. of boys rang saddening like a hymn 142

washing machine: stuck her head in a w. m. 72

whiskers: 'Runcible Cat with crimson w.!' 87

whiting: 'Will you walk a little faster?' said a w. to a snail 16

wind: Thy hair soft-lifted by the winnowing w. 46

winter: In w. I get up at night 49

wisdom: a five-haired beard of w. 26

wood: I went out to the hazel w. 174

world: When all the w. is young, lad 156

year: That time of y. thou mayst in me behold 95

young: And we were y. 135
When all the world is y., lad 156